PLAN B
Converting Change into Career Opportunity

Elwood N. Chapman

A FIFTY MINUTE™ SERIES BOOK

CRISP PUBLICATIONS, INC.
Menlo Park, California

PLAN B
Converting Change into Career Opportunity

Revised Edition

Elwood N. Chapman

CREDITS
Editor: **Michael G. Crisp**
Typesetting: **Interface Studio**
Cover Design: **Carol Harris**
Artwork: **Ralph Mapson**

Printed in the United States of America

Distribution to the U.S. Trade:

National Book Network, Inc.
4720 Boston Way
Lanham, MD 20706
1-800-462-6420

Library of Congress Catalog Card Number 92-054603
Chapman, Elwood N.
Plan B: Converting Change into Opportunity
ISBN 1-56052-195-3

This book is printed on recyclable paper with soy ink.

''Life is a series of collisions with the future; it is not a sum of what we have been but what we yearn to be.''

José Ortega y Gasset

ABOUT THIS BOOK

Plan B is not like most books. It stands out from others in an important way. It is not a book to read—it's a book to *use*. The unique "self-paced" format and the many exercises encourage the reader to get involved and try some new ideas immediately.

This publication will introduce innovative building-block ideas that will help you take advantage of your present job to dramatically enhance your future. Using the simple but sound system (seven steps) can head your career and life in a better direction. All you need do is give it a chance.

Plan B (and other titles listed in the back of this book) can be used effectively in a number of ways. Here are some possibilities.

—**Individual study.** Because the book is self-instructional, all that is needed is a quiet place, some time and a pencil. By completing the activities and exercises, most readers will quickly turn their present job into a stepping stone to a more progressive and exciting career path.

—**Workshops and Seminars.** The book is effective in helping participants unlock themselves from traditional but ineffective ways to view a job or career. By formulating a Plan B, one's Plan A starts to look better while other doors of opportunity open.

—**Resource for courses concerned with career progress.** Many teachers like to add a unit to their course content that will prepare students for the winds of change that exist in the world of work. The low cost of *Plan B* makes it possible for students to own their own copy.

Plan B is part of a series called *Be True to Your Future*. Other books include a Fifty-Minute *Career Discovery* program and a book titled *I Got The Job!* See the order form in the back of this book for more details.

PREFACE

The first edition of *Plan B* was published before the 1989 recession. Early birds, who took having a Plan B seriously, saved themselves from some of the trauma connected with major career adjustments that have since taken place. Today, five years later, a Plan B is considered by experts to be not only a smart move for those concerned with their future, but almost mandatory.

This second edition takes the momentous economic changes that have taken place in the last few years into consideration. It provides more in the way of updated strategies to help you convert change into opportunity as it protects your present career from the winds of change that continue to blow.

Once you understand the anatomy of a Plan B, chances are excellent you will initiate one for yourself and keep it in good working order until you reach retirement.

It *is* the smart thing to do!

Elwood N. Chapman

CONTENTS

VIEW YOUR CAREER FROM A NEW PERSPECTIVE

Erase from memory any preconceived ideas you have regarding career growth and job changes and open your mind to a new, innovative approach that will help you view your career from a more exciting perspective. A career growth program (Plan B), as conceived and introduced in this book, is far more than a contingency job plan. Rather, it is a thoughtful broad-based, personal growth program that can take you to either a more significant role in your present organization, or lead you to a better position elsewhere. It will also help you focus on a motivating life goal. Best of all, this can take place while you remain in your present job. The risk is minimal.

P A R T

I

LIFE GOALS COME FIRST

TIE YOUR HOPES TO A BIGGER STAR

The primary reason people lose motivation to succeed in their chosen careers is often because they do not link their efforts to a life goal. Without the advantage of a bigger picture, they become mired in an attitude best expressed by the old saying, ''another day another dollar.'' They become stalled and feel boxed in. Instead of viewing work as a vehicle that will lead them to fulfillment, they often see it as something to endure. Soon they are blaming their organization or their superiors for their lack of motivation.

Of course, when it comes to determining a life goal, it is easier said than done. Still, it need not be a frustrating, painful or lengthy process. In fact, with a little concentration, you can start the process now.

A good way to begin is to stop looking at your current job or position as simply a regular paycheck (with certain benefits) and view it instead as a vehicle that can take you in the direction you want to go in life. At first this may seem overwhelming, but all it really means is that you need to change the focus of your present thinking. In short, you can open and expand your mind and think bigger! Once you have a life goal, insights into what you can do to enhance your present career will improve and your motivation to succeed will be stronger and easier to maintain.

AIM HIGH

When Jane graduated from college she was excited about the future. When she landed a job as a marketing trainee with a national firm, she became even more enthusiastic. Three years later things turned sour. Jane felt bogged down and disenchanted. Soon she lost her self-motivation and became ineffective.

Why did it happen? Without knowing it, Jane had lost sight of her future. However, with the help of a close friend, she took time to reevaluate her dreams and focus on a life goal. Result? Jane developed a more professional perspective and regained her self-motivation. Not only did she get her confidence back, but everything she did was more directed and the improved quality of her work was noticed by all.

Please do not get the idea that you must develop a highly altruistic, euphoric life goal to get results similar to that of Jane. Very few individuals can make a significant scientific discovery, win a Nobel prize or be voted the most valuable player of a professional sports team. Your life goal will probably be a very practical thing like:

- raising a happy family
- building a dream home from scratch
- making other people happier with themselves
- achieving recognition through creative efforts
- creating an estate
- preparing for a fulfilling retirement

Everyone can develop a motivating life goal, but it is vital that you accept the premise that life goals differ from other goals. For example, selecting the right career or finding the best possible job is a significant accomplishment. However, these are not life goals. Buying a home is a worthy goal, but unless there are some special circumstances (like designing and building it yourself) it is not, for most people, a life goal.

YOUR LIFE GOALS

A life goal is usually expressed as something more personal that is beyond the framework of a job or career. The ideal life goal should provide inspiration over a life span. It should be a daily booster pump to one's attitude. A life goal can make challenges (like winning a promotion or finding a better job) easier to achieve. For those with a firm grip on a meaningful life goal, there is more spirit, substance and direction to daily living. And when times turn bad, they survive better.

BRINGING YOUR LIFE INTO FOCUS

Most people will not have as much trouble coming up with a life goal as they might expect. This is because, perhaps without knowing it, they already have one lying dormant within them. It is already *there* waiting to be brought to the surface. To help you discover a life goal, try asking yourself this question.

> WHAT DO I WANT TO ACCOMPLISH WITH THE TALENTS AND ABILITIES I POSSESS THAT WILL GIVE ME A SENSE OF LASTING FULFILLMENT?

Another approach is to project yourself into the future and imagine you are looking back on your life. Then ask yourself:

> WHAT WOULD HAVE GIVEN MY LIFE MORE MEANING?

GOALS SHOULD BE MOTIVATING

Although it may be ideal to think that a life goal must be worthy and contribute to humanity, this is not always true. Some goals, such as accumulating personal wealth or achieving power are not altruistic. Yet they can be life goals because they are highly motivating to some people over a life span.

No other person can define a life goal for you or impose one on you. Your goal must come from within and the choice is yours alone. Most of all, you must *want* to have one.

The following exercise was designed to help you isolate and clarify a life goal. It can do this by providing examples of how other people came up with their goals and how this discovery helped them enhance their careers. Please read the profiles. When you have finished, you are invited to project your own life goal at the end of the exercise. As you proceed, remember that minds are like parachutes–they don't function until they are open.

LIFE GOAL PROFILES

Listed below are examples that illustrate the significant relationship between life goals and career success. Please ☑ check the one with which you most closely identify and then write your own in the space provided at the end of this section.

☐ More than anything, Jake wants money. Having grown up lacking material goods, Jake sincerely wants financial security and, ultimately, an affluent lifestyle. So strong is his desire, that he intends to remain single until his goal is well on the way to reality. Although some of his friends consider Jake to be narrow-minded and selfish, his goal has kept him self-motivated over the past ten years. Result? Jake is now a vice president for a large accounting firm.

☐ Freda has two life goals woven into a single fabric. One is to travel, the other is to promote international understanding. Freda had to struggle over a long period of time to clarify her goals. As a result, she was almost 40 when she decided to go back to school. There she took travel courses and became bilingual. When she was ready to tackle the job market her life goal gave her the competitive edge to win an outstanding opportunity with the best travel agency in town. Since then, Freda has opened her own agency and has five agents working for her. She travels about 50 percent of the time and feels good about doing her small bit in promoting international understanding.

LIFE GOAL PROFILES

☐ Jennifer was going nowhere with her organization until she became a born-again Christian. Then, with more insight and motivation, she found a job that helped others become more self-sufficient. Today, even though her annual income is modest, she is challenged and happy. The difference? Jennifer claims it is because her goal to help others is being fulfilled. Her job is the vehicle that allows her to accomplish what is most important to her.

☐ When Matt and Joan ended their marriage, Joan's goal was to be a good parent and provider for her son Jimmy. With help from a college guidance center, she decided to prepare for and find a career in computer applications. Once started, it has been one career advance after another. What gave Joan the competitive advantage? Wanting to provide a good home for Jimmy made the difference.

☐ Raymond completed two years of college, did a hitch in the Marine Corps and worked part-time as a laborer for three years. He never gave much thought to something better. Then he met Sue. By the time they were engaged, he was working full time and on his way to becoming a journeyman carpenter. Raymond puts it this way: ''Once I wanted a future with Sue everything turned around for me. Someday I will be a contractor.''

LIFE GOAL PROFILES

DOING YOUR OWN PROFILE

The profiles of others you just read may help suggest the kind of profile you will eventually write for yourself. Now would be a good time to try writing a preliminary script for yourself, using the space below.

LIFE GOALS AND A PLAN B

Now that you have a better idea of what you want out of your life, having a Plan B makes more sense because it will keep you from getting stranded along the way. That is, if your present job (Plan A) is eliminated or you sense it is no longer leading you in the direction of your life goals, then you can activate your Plan B.

A Plan B is an alternative road that:

- Keeps you from getting ''boxed in''
- Strengthens your present position (Plan A)
- Prevents you from staying with a job that is leading you in the wrong direction, or in no direction at all
- Energizes you to keep up with changes
- Protects you and your family from the winds of change
- Makes you feel better about yourself
- Improves your attitude

PART

II

PLAN B AND THE WINDS OF CHANGE

LORI

When Lori first heard a friend of hers describe the psychological advantages of having a written Plan B, she was skeptical. To Lori, a Plan B was nothing more than a general plan to keep in the back of your mind in case you lost your job. Lori's friend persisted and Lori eventually won out. This is the way Lori now describes a Plan B:

"One of the 'laws of life' seems to be that the moment you don't have medical insurance, you break your leg; when you don't have auto insurance, you have an accident. I view having a Plan B in the same way. When you have the job security that only an alternative growth program can provide, chances are good you won't need it. But having the protection provides a sense of confidence. It is nice to feel you don't really need another job but know you are ready if things change. It comes down to what insurance people call 'risk management.' By protecting your future, it creates a whole different attitude toward your present work."

WHAT IS A PLAN B?

A Plan B as described in this book is a carefully researched and designed strategy to provide an immediate and exciting career opportunity should your present job (Plan A) lose its luster or disappear. A Plan B is not a temporary alternative or substitute job should problems arise. It is a reserve program that can match or be superior to your Plan A (present job). Properly developed, it will provide a cushion against the shocks of future changes, such as unexpected unemployment.

View a completed Plan B as having a large sum of money salted away in an investment of your choice. Or, if you prefer, a paid-up insurance policy. You may never draw on the account (or cash in the insurance policy) but if necessary, you know you have a back-up program. And, just as well-invested money draws interest or pays dividends while held in reserve, so does a Plan B. For example, the very existence of a Plan B growth program can cause you to feel more independent (and secure) about your present job. This, in turn, can cause you to be more confident and thereby do better at it. It can also give your present job (whatever it may be) more meaning and help you make progress toward a life goal. These, and other significant benefits to be explored in the pages ahead, are not normally seen or understood. But they exist and can guarantee that you receive a high rate of interest from your investment. In other words, a Plan B growth program will add new assets to your ''career bank.''

Despite these and other advantages, most people wait on the sidelines without developing a diversified career contingency plan. In doing this, they put all of their career eggs into one basket. This is foolish when you consider that a Plan B can help a Plan A prosper.

THE ANATOMY OF A PLAN B

A Plan B is a comprehensive, detailed and realistic career plan that can be activated within a few days. It is a seven-step strategy that has been planned in advance so if your present job (Plan A) disappears, or you wish to leave it behind, you have replacement choices. These will be in harmony with your abilities, talents, interests and life goals.

A Plan B growth program is more than an idea in the back of your mind. It must be fully researched and planned in writing. Key contacts must also be developed as your Plan B is formulated. Although it may sound like doing a homework assignment, it is far more exciting and the benefits are greater and more immediate. Ideally, your Plan B can be developed while you are improving your Plan A. Many successful people devote several hours each week over a period of months to develop and refine a high-quality Plan B.

And they enjoy the challenge!

THE WINDS OF CHANGE

For many people, a Plan B would have been a good idea twenty years ago. But, then, few people were thinking in that direction. Ten years ago such a plan would have been an excellent strategy. Those who developed one outdistanced others. Today Plan B is virtually mandatory. Those who read the daily paper or watch TV soon realize there is no immunity from changes that can render either your job or your organization obsolete.

What our parents used to call a secure job is extinct. Changes have been so dramatic in recent years that even if you own and operate a small business, economic, social, political or legal changes can suddenly throw you into bankruptcy. Perhaps trends change, or maybe rent or insurance rates explode. Life simply doesn't come with guarantees.

Alvin Toffler, in his book *Future Shock* (published in 1971), predicted changes that seemed revolutionary. Many of the changes he predicted arrived so fast that Mr. Toffler published a second book soon thereafter titled *The Third Wave* to catch up on the wild winds of change. Toffler did an outstanding job describing the large changes to the country. Most people were unable, however, to consider how those changes would affect their lives. Only a few individuals took Toffler's predictions personally.

In addition to external changes (such as those described by Toffler), there are changes within individuals. Sometimes a person reaches a crisis point where a new life goal appears and career adjustments need to be made. At other times, job dissatisfaction becomes acute and a change becomes a necessity.

Are the winds of change blowing in your life today? What impact will they have on your future? On the following pages are some causes (winds) that may sweep you off your feet.

Are you ready for them?

WINDS THAT COULD BLOW YOUR JOB AWAY

RESTRUCTURING: Almost all major organizations are streamlining to lower overhead and become more competitive. World competition for established markets is responsible. Some organizations started this process earlier than others. They were wise. The result for these organizations was more gradual change and fewer layoffs. Today, no organization is immune. Everyone has had to adjust. Some firms have helped retrain employees for new jobs; others have simply cut their workforce. This downsizing has had a sobering effect upon employee morale. Some of the more fortunate employees received special severance incentives (known as golden handshakes) or were provided with professional outplacement counseling to help them adjust. Others were simply handed a pink slip and left to fend for themselves. Very few of those laid-off had a workable Plan B in the wings.

MERGERS: In a merger, two organizations decide to join forces to become more efficient or enter new markets. Often one company is in financial trouble and is taken over by a healthy corporation. The term often used during a merger is consolidation. Savings occur when two offices are combined into one. But people pay the price because two sets of employees, such as office staff, are not usually needed. Someone has to go or change jobs and seniority or talent do not always count.

RECESSION: The recession that started in 1989 continues in many sections of the United States. Unemployment remains high. The downsizing of corporations continues. The reduction of officers and enlisted personnel in all branches of the military is accelerating. In some areas of our economy, the winds of change are blowing harder than ever. Until the United States pulls itself out of the recession, the need for a Plan B will be greater than ever.

CHANGES—CHANGES—CHANGES

DISLOCATIONS: Economic pressures sometimes make it necessary for an organization to relocate its offices or plants. Sometimes organizations move from places such as New York or California because of high salaries and rent to less expensive places such as Texas or Kentucky. It makes good sense economically, but in the process many people are left behind. Often many can't (or won't) move. They resist the winds of change. If they do not have a Plan B in reserve, they must scramble.

POLITICAL: Everyone is familiar with political change. In Washington, D.C., smart people always have a Plan B. Partisan employees face the strongest political winds. Civil service provides job security, but even here changes are being considered. Political winds accelerate economic and social changes that can affect everyone.

SOCIAL: Double income families are more vulnerable to change than when there is a single wage earner. If the primary breadwinner loses his or her job, it often means this person has to find suitable employment elsewhere. Result? Two people need a Plan B rather than one. Social winds have indirectly created a greater need for alternative career plans.

All of the winds of change mentioned add up to a compelling need for smart workers to have a well-designed Plan B. It is no longer *if* you get caught up on the whirlwind of change that might result in a change in your job status, it is being prepared for *when*.

JULIE

Julie was so tired of rumors about cutbacks that there was a certain amount of relief when her firm finally declared bankruptcy and eliminated her position. She immediately signed up for unemployment insurance payments and took a two-week "vacation." Then she started a job hunting expedition.

Things didn't go well. For one thing, Julie wasn't prepared mentally for a job search. Even worse, she had allowed some of her basic skills to deteriorate. As a result, Julie became discouraged and lost her confidence. It took her over a year (including several college classes) to get her once-promising career back on track.

Julie made the classic mistake of thinking she could use unemployment insurance as a security blanket. She felt a new job would be easy to find. What she failed to understand is that developing a Plan A from scratch is far more difficult than developing a Plan B while you are still working. If Julie had worked on a feasible growth program before her position was eliminated, she could have enjoyed her vacation and returned prepared to locate a better position than she left. With a solid Plan B her one year "down period" would have been eliminated.

If you dislike trying to find a job on a full-time basis, a growth program prepared ahead of time is your best possible strategy.

REDUCTION OF FULL-TIME POSITIONS WITH COMPREHENSIVE BENEFITS

All of the changes taking place are making the traditional full-time job (with comprehensive benefits) more difficult to hang on to and more difficult to find. Some experts anticipate that over ten percent of existing full-time positions will be replaced by part-time jobs by the turn of the century. Here some other workforce changes that are anticipated.

- Due to the disappearance of full-time positions, more and more college graduates will, by necessity, start their careers in part-time internship roles.
- Over 30 percent of all jobs will be part-time or temporary in nature.
- Free-lancing will continue to expand.
- "Temps" (those who are employed and assigned by agencies) will fill in during peak periods to reduce the number of full-timers employed.
- Entrepreneurship will grow.

All of these changes send a clear signal that there will be more movement within the workforce and that having a Plan B will become increasingly important. The old days where a college graduate was encouraged to find a large firm with good benefits and settle in to climb the executive ladder for thirty years is over. Today the signal is to find the best job available (full or part-time) and immediately prepare a Plan B so that the graduate can take advantage of opportunities as they surface.

PLAN B BEGINS WITH A PHILOSOPHY

It would be a mistake to consider a career growth program (prepared while in your present job) simply as a blueprint to take you through a difficult transition period into another job or career. It is equally important to view such a plan as an attitude. The mind-set for Plan B says one must not depend exclusively on others (especially managers in large organizations) to develop and protect your future. A good Plan B is a ''take care of yourself'' project. It is an attitude that acknowledges change is inevitable and no job or career is 100 percent secure. It is an attitude that recognizes the danger in becoming too comfortable with any career role and the acceptance that alternatives are necessary to avoid becoming vulnerable to the winds of change.

Obviously, change can be a barrier from reaching a life goal. Change can send a person on a detour from which a return to the main highway is difficult. Thus, a Plan B philosophy says: ''No matter how strong the winds may be, you cannot allow them to blow away your future. You must ride out the storm, adjust, and be true to your future.''

Plan B is basically a way to interpret the modern world, which will give you a better chance to reach your life goals. The ''good old days'' of company loyalty, and promotion from within, are not as realistic as they once were. The rules have changed. The game is played differently. And, without a Plan B, you risk leaving yourself open to frustration and despair.

The good news about constructing a career growth program is that the philosophy you develop will enhance other aspects of your life. Some examples of this are provided on the next page.

THE PLAN B HABIT

Some years ago my wife and I were traveling in Europe when student riots in France prevented us from following our scheduled plan. Stranded in London, and feeling sorry for ourselves, we came up with an alternate plan to visit Scotland. We had a glorious time and that experience caused us to form the Plan B habit.

Although the material in this book deals with the benefits of developing a career Plan B (and how to do it), you will also see the advantages in other situations. For example, a Plan B is desirable:

- When a financial reverse occurs
- When another individual lets you down
- When unexpected company arrives
- When a college major turns sour
- When your dentist retires
- When your favorite restaurant is closed
- When a computer fails
- When your car breaks down
- When your flight is cancelled

Almost every plan you make could use a Plan B to provide flexibility and prevent frustration. In developing a Plan B for career and life goal purposes, you will see the advantages (and improve your skills) in having a backup strategy in every day situations. Result? The unexpected bumps of living will be easier to handle.

HAVING A PLAN A, B, C AND D

In discussing the strategy of having a Plan A and B, you often hear people say facetiously that the winds of change are blowing so powerfully that one needs a Plan A, B, C and D. This may not be such a bad idea! For example, let's view Dale as a hypothetical case and take him through the possibility of four plans.

PLAN A

Dale has an excellent full-time job with good benefits. She would like to think that her job is 100 percent secure but she knows this is not the case. Even if she does her best (Dale is considered to be an outstanding employee with high potential) there is a possibility her firm will merge with another or make other internal changes so that her present job may no longer be necessary. Dale likes her Plan A, she wants to keep her Plan A, but Dale also knows it is smart to have a Plan B.

PLAN B

Dale is ambitious and wants to retire at age fifty-five. If promotions do not come fast enough under her Plan A, she may activate her Plan B. Dale has devoted hours to its preparation. She does everything possible to improve her professional skills and she stays in touch with other professionals in her career specialty. With a resume that is always updated and a fine reputation created through networking, Dale is always looking for a better opportunity. She does this despite the fact that she is happy with her Plan A. As Dale puts it, "Having a Plan B prepares me to take advantage of any career opportunities that come my way. If I can find a better job elsewhere, I'll take it."

PLAN C

What if the winds of change take an extremely negative turn for Joe? What if he lost his Plan A job and things turned so bad that his Plan B won't work for a few months or a year? Joe's Plan C is to open up a business of his own where he could continue to employ his professional specialty. Joe already knows the kind of business he would like to operate. He has set aside enough capital to get it started. Now and then he works part-time (moonlighting) in a business similar to the one he would start up, in the event his Plan A and Plan B fall apart. Joe says this about his Plan C, "I keep my Plan C on a back burner. Hopefully, I won't need it until I am ready to retire. But if I should become disenchanted working for others, I might change my mind and activate it sooner."

PLAN D

Joe's Plan D is a fall-back plan that he hopes he will never need to employ. The plan consists of drawing unemployment insurance, while he continues to update his Plans B and C, until he activates one plan or the other. In other words, if Joe lost in Plan A (present job), could not put his well-prepared Plan B into effect due to a recession or his own ill health, and felt that his Plan C (starting his own business) was not wise, then Joe would fall back to his Plan D on a *temporary* basis. It would be a plan of last resort, designed to give Joe time to adjust his Plan B to new market conditions or initiate his Plan C.

Obviously, with a Plan A, B, C and D, Joe is ready for the future. Notice that Joe is aware of the maintenance features of his plans. They are not just plans that Joe keeps in his head or a file drawer, they are plans that he constantly works at and updates. In other words, it is looking at all contingencies and staying ahead of competitors in his professional career field.

THOSE WITH A PLAN B IN PLACE USUALLY WIND UP HAPPIER IN THE WORKPLACE AND LESS SUSCEPTIBLE TO JOB BURNOUT

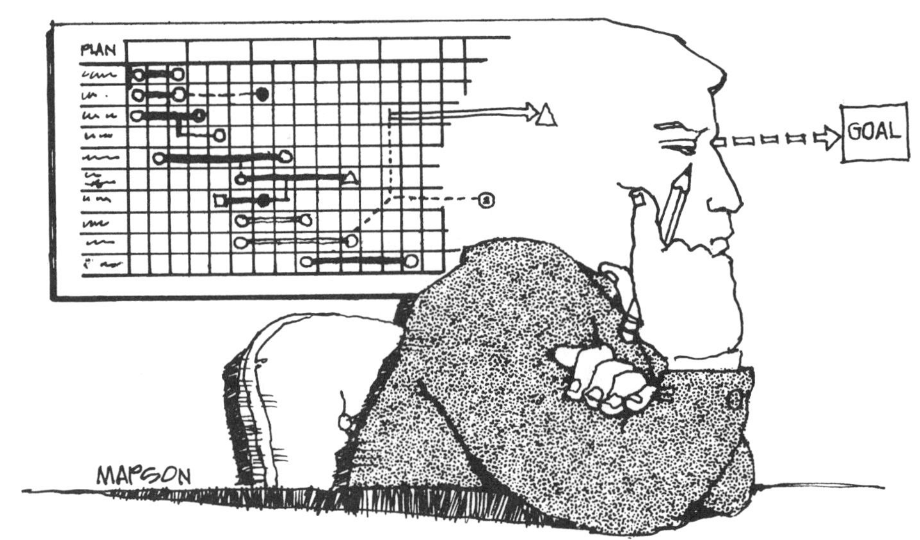

THE CHALLENGE!

The foundation of the Plan B philosophy is the development of a learning attitude that says: "I will start learning more about my specific career area and the opportunities it provides from a variety of sources. These sources include key people I know or will meet in the future. It means learning more about my present job, including attending seminars and self-learning. I accept that only by keeping my skills current can I avoid a major catch-up period in the future—a period that could measurably slow my career progress.

P A R T

III

THE SEVEN-STEP STRATEGY

ANTICIPATING THE WINDS OF CHANGE

This section contains seven steps that will lead you through a successful Plan B growth program. Although all seven steps are recommended, you may decide to eliminate one or two or place more emphasis on some. Every situation is different. Each individual has his or her own form of interpretation and style. After all, the future you are dealing with is your own!

THE SEVEN-STEP STRATEGY

STEP 1 COMMIT YOURSELF

(Here you will design a support system to help you complete a Plan B.)

Few individuals who promise themselves to complete a growth plan actually do so, because they lack a support system. Without such a system, it is easy for a Plan B to become ''just talk.''

> Genevieve had slowly turned off her friends and co-workers through constant talk about getting a teaching credential, but never doing anything about it. Her best friend, Rachel, finally decided to address the situation and said: ''Look, Gen, we are all tired of talk without any action. Why don't you do something about your future or forget it? I'll make you a wager. When you get your credential I'll buy you dinner at the best restaurant in town. Between now and then, promise you won't keep talking about how you're going to get your credential. Deal?''

Like Genevieve, most people need all the motivation they can muster to start and complete a Plan B. What kind of motivation would you require? And equally important, what kind of support from others would be necessary to convert what is in your mind to action? On the next page are four options. If you feel that one is the kind of support you would favorably respond to, place a check in the appropriate square. If none appeals to you, design your own plan in the space provided.*

*Should the reader feel that a support system of any kind is unnecesary, he or she is reminded that a Plan B must be developed while a Plan A is kept in full operation and one's lifestyle is maintained. It is something you do on top of everything else. It is not business as usual and that is why an advance support strategy (especially if there is some excitement to it) may be best for some people.

DESIGN A SUPPORT SYSTEM

☐ **Option #1: USE THE POWER OF SECRECY.** For some individuals, getting others to provide support would demonstrate weakness on their part and do more harm than good. These people like to prove to others, (especially superiors), that they are independently strong and disciplined. Thus, the more secrecy surrounding the project, the more motivated these individuals become. It is the fact that they do not discuss their Plan B with others until they can make a big announcement at the end (after completion) that provides the motivating goal.

☐ **Option #2: COMMIT YOURSELF TO OTHERS.** This option is in juxtaposition to number one. Some individuals find the motivation they require is obtained by openly communicating their plan to those most important in their lives. Not having to back down from a commitment (and winding up with the guilt) is what causes these people to complete a project. They purposely create their own trap and then make certain they are not caught in it!

☐ **Option #3: ARRANGE A PERSONAL CONTRACT.** This works when there is a significant person who is willing to provide support and counseling on a regular basis. Spouses, close friends, or mentors work well. The idea is to make a verbal (or written) agreement to meet at regular intervals to evaluate progress until the Plan B is complete. For many individuals, this options works well.

☐ **Option #4: CHOOSE A SMALL, SELECT SUPPORT GROUP.** Those who prefer this approach like to share their Plan B with a select group of individuals who can be called upon for guidance and support. It is like doing a long-distance swim and having people at both ends and along your side to cheer you on as you make the effort. Structure in the form of regular progress reports can be added if desired. Here again, care in the selection of support people is critical. Only those who will take the assignment seriously should be given consideration.

☐ **Option #5: DOING IT WITH OTHERS.** For some, a partnership or team arrangement is the best of all. Besides the fun that can occur sharing and working together, mutual support is nice to have. The primary problem with a partnership approach is that one party may be more serious and professional than the other to produce a viable Plan B. A team or partnership effort might work, but it would be wise to reserve one of the other options in case is doesn't.

☐ **Option #6: SELF-DESIGNED STRATEGY.** Please write out the option you prefer. If desired, use a combination of those suggested above.

____

____

____

____

____

____

Once you have your support system in place you are ready to prepare a Plan B for launching at a later date. The more you anticipate this event, the more motivated you will be to get there!

My personal goal for step 1 is to employ Option # ____________

CASE 1: RICHARD

When Richard came home from Viet Nam, it was his Uncle George who introduced him to the president of Barr Manufacturing, who offered Richard a job. Since then Richard has made slow but steady progress with Barr. He is now traffic manager (and loves it) but is worried for two reasons. (1) He needs to measurably upgrade his statistical skills to keep the job. (2) Rumor has it that Barr may sell out to a larger company.

Richard has been thinking about developing a Plan B for two years but lacks enough motivation to get started. Last night, in a discussion with his wife Marie, it was decided he should adopt one of these strategies.

(1) Ask Uncle George if he will sign an informal contract that commits Richard to report on his progress every two weeks. Richard has so much respect for his uncle that it would be very difficult to let him down. Besides, Uncle George is knowledgeable and could provide expert guidance until his Plan B is finished.

(2) Create a small support group by asking the following individuals if they would be available to talk with him should his progress bog down.

- –Marie
- –His superior at work, with whom he has a mentor-type relationship
- –Jack, his best friend
- –Neighbor Fred, who is a retired teacher
- –Uncle George

Which strategy would you support?

____

____

____

See page 85 for author's comments.

STEP 2
DO BETTER AT YOUR PRESENT JOB

(Free yourself to do a Plan B by streamlining your Plan A.)

Frequently an individual will fix up a home or automobile to sell, then, after the improvements have been made, change his or her mind. The home or car turns out to be better than what is available for the same price in the marketplace. Why not keep it?

The same thing can happen in preparing a growth plan. When you have finished with it, your Plan A (present job) looks so much better than when you started you decide to keep it. This is most apt to occur when you streamline your Plan A to work on Plan B.

> When Jill first heard a friend say the best way to get ready to leave a job is to become better at it, she almost flipped. Yet, after discussing the idea at length, Jill agreed. The premise is basic. By becoming more effective at Plan A, it ceases to be a drag on the preparation of a Plan B. Then, if Plan B does not work out, you can fall back on an improved Plan A and still come out ahead. Some people call this hedging. Jill decided to follow this strategy.

It stands to reason that developing a workable Plan B will take time, energy and mental effort. But does it need to be a burden? The answer is no, providing you relieve some of the pressure by becoming more effective in your present job. In other words, streamline what you do so you become more efficient and it takes less out of you.

As contradictory as it may at first seem, your second step is to improve the way you are dealing with your Plan A. To assist you in doing this, twenty possible efficiency measures are listed on the next page. It is recognized that work situations are vastly different, so some of the suggestions may not apply.

IMPROVING YOUR PLAN A

Read each of the following statements, then place a check in the box opposite those that you are willing to accomplish.

- ☐ Curtail excessive socialization on your present job (Plan A). Stay friendly with co-workers but concentrate more on the job itself.
- ☐ Concentrate on your job and let others worry about problems beyond your control.
- ☐ Become more professional as a worker. Look and act the part.
- ☐ Become a more positive person. Let negative views and rumors bounce off you.
- ☐ Work hard to increase personal productivity. A drop in your productivity can be counterproductive in building a Plan B.
- ☐ Work to restore any negative relationships that exist. These cause an energy drain that could be put to better use elsewhere.
- ☐ Eliminate obvious time-wasters that have become habits (such as personal telephone calls).
- ☐ Insulate yourself against unsolvable human problems that are draining you.
- ☐ Do a better job of balancing home and career responsibilities.
- ☐ If you are a manager, start delegating more. If you are not a manager, spend less time carrying the work load of others.
- ☐ Take a stronger stand with superiors on accepting new responsibilities. Refuse to let others unload on you. Carry your full share of work but take a firm stand against overloads.

IMPROVING YOUR PLAN A (Continued)

☐ Use your lunch break (or other down time) to work on Plan B.

☐ Start building stronger relationships with those who may be in a position to help you launch your Plan B later.

☐ Start an exercise program.

☐ Improve your absentee record.

☐ Establish (in writing) daily work priorities.

☐ Whatever it takes to build a better relationship with your supervisor, do it. The less strain that falls on you from above, the easier the building of your Plan B will be.

☐ Shorten business telephone conversations.

☐ Dress for success. Looking more efficient may help you become more efficient.

Your goal is to develop a Plan B that will improve your career, get you a better job and take you closer to your life goal. With less stress coming from your Plan A you will be free to do this and improve your future.

If it sounds like too much work, talk it over with a support person. Perhaps there is some way you can convert the streamlining you have in mind to a challenge with a reward at the end.

I intend to take a fresh look at my present job. In addition to accomplishing those items checked, my basic goal in step 2 is to ______________________________

____

____

CASE 2: CONFLICT

Although James and Gregg are good friends they occasionally get into some highly emotional arguments over career strategies. Yesterday, over lunch, they had a beauty when Gregg said.

> "James, you might as well quit now, take a vacation, and come back looking for a new job. You miss the whole idea of using your present job as a platform to gain a better one. You can't seem to get it through your brain that becoming better at what you are doing here will improve your attitude toward outside opportunities. Right now you are cutting off your nose to spite your face."
>
> "Look big shot," replied James, "you don't know how negative I have become about this job. I feel I am in a pressure cooker and management is turning the gas higher. Then, you sit there and tell me to take a fresh look at what I am dong to benefit myself. My guess is that 95 percent of people who turn sour on a job quit without having a decent plan. That's the way the system works. The only way I am going to benefit myself is to quit and take that vacation you are talking about. I will never prepare for another job until the pressure is totally off me here. As far as I am concerned, you can take your Plan B and stuff it in your ear."

Would you defend James or Gregg? Write your answer in the space below and then compare your answers to that of the author on page 85.

____

____

____

STEP 3
LEARN MORE FROM WHERE YOU ARE

(Your present job can provide more than money or benefits while you work on your Plan B.)

This step encourages you to view your current job as a place where you can continue to learn. This holds true even if you feel boxed in, or mad at your boss, or even if you don't expect to hang around for long.

Some employees become so discouraged about their current jobs that they do not recognize some of the on-site learning opportunities that are present. A few, once they become serious about a Plan B, take a second look and discover a wide variety of learning opportunities exist. When this happens, they often reverse their previous attitude and start improving old skills while learning new ones. Of course, this doesn't happen to everyone. Rather than viewing their Plan A as a paid learning station for the duration (the smart approach), some people continue to see it as a bummer job leading nowhere. These individuals needlessly victimize themselves.

Improving and streamlining your Plan A (Step 2) may have already contributed to a more positive attitude toward your current job and this may have uncovered some learning opportunities you have failed to see in the past. If so, step in and learn all you can. Continue to search for new assignments and new relationships with people who have something important to teach you. The more you learn, the better things will turn out for you in the future. Easy to say, hard to do!

PSYCHOLOGICAL BLOCKS

One reason you may not have taken advantage of learning opportunities in the past is because you may have some psychological blocks to overcome. For example, blocks frequently occur among mature employees in a high tech field (like computer science). These individuals are fully capable of learning new technology but have permitted the never-ending advancement of technology to form barriers in their mind and they give up.

There are three steps to overcoming learning blocks: (1) Recognize you may have one. (2) Make up your mind to reverse the problem. (3) Find help to master what needs to be learned.

There is another kind of mental block. When a change occurs in the work environment, some employees always seem to consider it bad no matter what the change may be. As a result, they develop a negative attitude (mental block) against it. Other colleagues have learned to view change as an opportunity, not a problem. This attitude allows them to open their minds, learn new methods or skills and prepare for better jobs ahead. These individuals are not just putting in time, they are preparing themselves for the future.

What can you learn from your present job? It depends upon where you are, the freedom you have and what new learning opportunities surround you. Sometimes, after careful analysis, you may discover your job environment may not provide any new learning opportunities despite your best effort. If this turns out to be the case, you should move on to step 5.

LEARNING SOURCES

To help you identify learning sources from your present job, please complete the following exercise. Place a ☑ opposite any learning opportunity that can be developed.

☐ Ask your supervisor for some new responsibilities where learning possibilities exist. One idea is to start with a task co-workers do not want.

☐ Go on record requesting to learn how to operate a piece of equipment or software, where you have little or no experience. Sometimes it is possible to learn this on your own time.

☐ Investigate the opportunities of company sponsored seminars or training that you can attend or take.

☐ Ask a colleague who is a specialist to help you develop some new skills.

☐ Identify accessible individuals whom you can learn from through informal meetings, interviews and coffee breaks. Some people are better resources than books.

Each work environment has its own learning opportunities. All it takes is a motivated person who is willing to discover and absorb knowledge. This usually means asking the right questions at the right time of the right people. Although formal education and self-learning outside of work will also contribute to your future, there is nothing that can replace the on-the-job training and experience most organizations provide.

My goal is to learn the following processes (skills) from my current job within the next sixty days:

____________________ ____________________

____________________ ____________________

____________________ ____________________

CASE 3: ATTITUDE REVERSAL

When Tanya started with her firm two years ago she made some serious mistakes. First, she learned only what was necessary for her to get the basic job done. Nothing extra. Second, she made some unnecessary human relation errors. As a result, she is currently at odds with her supervisor and has a serious conflict with two co-workers. Because she got herself off to such a bad start, Tanya has decided to develop a Plan B.

Tanya's first move was to start taking advantage of learning opportunities she neglected in the past. This included qualifying to operate three pieces of office equipment with which she was unfamiliar. She also recognized a need for greater concentration on her English skills to reduce her level of mistakes. Finally, Tanya decided to work hard to improve her relationship with her supervisor and co-workers. Tanya admits that doing all of this will mean a major behavioral change on her part, but she views it as an integral part of developing a Plan B. Besides, it is never too late to change.

What success do you predict for Tanya?

☐ Tanya will become discouraged and leave her job before her Plan B is complete.

☐ Tanya will succeed and after her Plan B is complete she will move on to a much better job.

To compare your views to that of the author, please turn to page 85.

STEP 4
IMPROVE YOUR PRESENT SKILLS

(Then and only then are you officially in the race.)

In most athletic contests (cycling races, 10K's, swimming events, etc.), one must qualify to compete for the recognition and prizes offered. The same is true in the career race. To qualify, a person must verify and reach current job skill standards. Those who do not do this may *think* they are in the race, but the truth is they have disqualified themselves before starting.

Every job specialty has its own competency standards. A competency is nothing more than a skill that can be observed and measured. There are technical skills *and* human relations skills. Although human relations skills are not as easy to quantify as technical skills, they are equally important.

The problem with job competencies in a dynamic society is that they are constantly upgraded by the job market. Professionals understand this and strive to keep their skills up to standard or above. Nonprofessionals allow their competencies to slip.

Both Hazel and Florence use applications software in their positions as financial analysts. Hazel has a great attitude toward learning. Through self-instruction and formal classes she keeps current with the newest software. Florence has a get-by learning attitude. She depends greatly on the help of others to keep her job.

If both of their jobs should be eliminated, Hazel would be "market ready" for another job. Florence would not.

WHERE ARE YOU?

Where are you? Do you need to do a market skills analysis to see if you have fallen behind in your specialty? If so, this effort should be a part of your Plan B program. To assist you in doing this, the following three-part strategy is recommended.

FIRST Write out what you believe to be the present competencies required to keep you competitive in your job speciality. Include both technical and human skills.

VERIFY

NEXT Verify your list by consulting with placement or human resource professionals (your local college counselor can help direct you to such a person). This, in effect, will constitute a skill analysis. Add new competencies you need to learn. Delete those no longer required.

THEN Make a list of any competencies where upgrading is required to make you competitive.

____

____

____

____

____

____

____

My overall goal for step 4 is to ☐ earn a promotion with my present firm; ☐ qualify for a better position in the open market; ☐ both.

COMMENTS: ________________________________

____

____

____

CASE 4: JACK'S PROBLEM

When Jack finally got around to verifying the skills he would need to compete effectively for a job that was consistant with his life goal, he realized just how far behind he was. He knew some upgrading was due when he started, but when he took a close look at his list, Jack was tempted to give up.

Then it occured to him that he had two options. His first option would be to divide the competencies he needed into three groups. In Group 1 Jack would include those skills he could learn from his present job; Group 2 would include those competencies he could learn from self-study efforts at home; Group 3 would include those that he could learn only from more formal training, probably from evening courses at the local college.

His second option would be to quit his present job and return to campus full time. In this manner he could catch up more quickly and then start over with a new job. This option would put a strain on Jack's finances and curtail his lifestyle but would not be impossible.

What other factors should Jack consider in making his decision? Which option would you recommend? Why?

Compare your thinking with the author's on page 85.

STEP 5
BACK TO SCHOOL? SELF-INSTRUCTION? BOTH?

(What choice will you make?)

When it comes to reaching new competency goals in order to maintain market mobility, most people have a choice. They can either go on campus (enroll in a night program) or undertake a self-instructional program at home. Once you have given careful consideration to the factors below, you are invited to make the decision that is best for you.

FORMAL TRAINING AS A BRIDGE TO PLAN B

Most people find it necessary or advisable to obtain academic preparation to reach their Plan B. Sometimes (as in obtaining a license to practice medicine) this preparation can take years. Some professions require a degree to qualify for entry. At other times, a single course can do the trick.

Consider the following cases.

Jason's Plan B is to become a second-level manager for a state agency. So far, Jason has taken advantage of every in-service training program available. He also asks for additional responsibilities when there are some learning opportunities involved. But Jason faces a serious problem in the future because he cannot speak Spanish. Increasingly, co-workers and clients are Hispanic. Two weeks ago Jason enrolled in Spanish I at a local community college. He knows reaching his Plan B depends upon his becoming bilingual.

Six years ago Joan was a secretary in an architectural firm. Today she is an architect in the same organization. Developing a Plan B is responsible for the transition. Joan realized her career at that firm was at a dead-end. Six years ago, she started fooling with a Plan B and, as a result, took a course called Architecture I at a local state college. The instructor was so enthusiastic and understanding that Joan became hooked. With the full cooperation of her firm, she completed the total curriculum. Academic training was her bridge between being a secretary and an architect.

Beth (a salesperson in a department store) and her husband Ken (a bank manager) designed a program to establish a small business of their own. Their academic preparation consisted of taking a college course at night called Successful Small Business Operation. The course project consisted of setting up a hypothetical business on paper. The professor allowed Beth and Ken to work as a team. When the course was over Beth quit her job first to get things started while Ken's salary continued. Ken joined Beth after two years. Although the academic training was minimal, without it Beth and Ken would not have received the necessary foundation to establish a successful business.

DO-IT-YOURSELF LEARNING

Self-study is a growing way to reach competency goals contained in a Plan B. Michelle is a case in point.

> Michelle has just about exhausted the learning opportunities in her present job. Because she is a single parent raising two children, she cannot easily attend courses at the local university. She has not, however, lost her enthusiasm for her Plan B. Two or three nights each week, after the children are in bed. Michelle devotes a minimum of one hour to her own self-development. She selects publications that will lead in the direction of her Plan B. Currently she is taking a correspondence course in Beginning Supervision. Michelle's goal is to become an administrative officer in the small school district where she is employed.
>
> In discussing her self-development program with her boss, Michelle made this statement: ''Reading and studying self-help books fits into my lifestyle. After the day is over and there is some quiet time, I can sit down with a cup of coffee and make excellent progress. Sometimes I can apply what I have learned the following day. My future plans do not call for an academic degree but, if needed in the future, I can list in my résumé the self-help subjects covered just as if I had attended a class. Some people who find it impossible to attend formal college classes give up on future progress. This is foolish. Self-learning has many advantages. You pick your own subjects and set your own pace. Of course, it takes self-discipline but what kind of education doesn't?''

All you need do is visit your local public library or a commercial book store and browse through the various self-help books that are available for your consideration. As an example, the publisher of this book specializes in self-study books. A list of those titles can be found at the back of the book.

My basic goal in step 5 is to: ______________________________________

____

____

IT IS POSSIBLE TO DO BOTH!

Of course, some individuals (in addition to what they learn on the job), return to campus for courses and engage in self-instructional programs at the same time. These people wisely design their own curriculum to meet their specific goals. As a guide to your own educational program please complete the following:

I plan to return to campus to complete these courses:

____

____

____

____

I plan to use self-help publications to upgrade myself in these areas:

____

____

____

____

Lifelong learning has become a reality. To those in retirement, learning for the sake of learning is an enviable attitude; for those who remain in the workplace, new learning is often a necessity. The winds of change dictate the curriculum.

IT IS A MISTAKE TO ASSUME YOUR PRESENT COMPETENCIES WILL TAKE YOU ALL THE WAY TO RETIREMENT

CASE 5: A CHALLENGE FOR MARY

Mary accepted a position as a clerk/receptionist with a major supermarket organization because it was the only job immediately available when her husband started a new legal practice. Mary figures the Liberal Arts degree she had would stand her in good stead even though her clerical skills were underdeveloped.

Mary soon became intrigued with the marketing department and decided her creative talents could be put to good use in that area. As a receptionist, she knew Ralph Dillon, vice president in charge of marketing. One morning, as Mr. Dillon entered the building, she asked if she could speak with him. He gave her a time to meet. The meeting determined the following skills that Mary would need to achieve before she would be a candidate to join the marketing department.

- High–level knowledge of applications software
- More graphics experience in layout and design
- A course in market research
- Better understanding of coupon marketing
- A course on consumer behavior

Overwhelmed by the list, Mary decided to think twice about the idea. A few days later, Mr. Dillion saw Mary and said, "You would already have some of the skills we discussed had you been a marketing major, but frankly, I like the creativity of your liberal arts background. All of the skills we listed can be learned at night at our local university or through some self-help materials I can provide. Are you still interested?"

Does this constitute a good Plan B for Mary? What suggestions would you make as far as implementation? Please write out your answers and compare with those on page 86.

STEP 6
CREATIVE NETWORKING: GET STARTED TODAY

(Sometimes who you know can be as important as what you know.)

Although placement agencies have helped thousands of people, never forget that the best strategy is to depend upon yourself. Translated, this means you should think of yourself as your own employment agency. There are employers who are seeking people with certain skills. Just like an employment agency, you will gain your best results by marketing yourself through creative networking.

You have a major advantage over others because you soon will have completed a Plan B. Although you may not have thought about it, your plan can constitute the secret formula you need. The following four strategies will help you establish your own employment agency.

INVITATION

APPENDIX I, PAGE 87, WILL ASSIST YOU IN RATING YOUR CURRENT JOB-GETTING SKILLS. PLEASE TAKE TEN MINUTES TO COMPLETE THIS EXERCISE. DOING THIS WILL BE A GREAT HELP WHEN YOU ARE READY TO LAUNCH YOUR PLAN B.

FOR THOSE NEW TO NETWORKING

Networking involves building relationships with knowledgeable professionals in your career area of interest who are in a position to lead you to a new and better job opportunity. You may include placement directors on your networking list but most should be people in the field to which you aspire. Some may be in your present company. Others may work for competitors.

Relationships you build should be mutually rewarding. This means you must look for ways to repay them (if only in gratitude) so they are willing to go out of their way to assist you.

Building such a network should start as early as possible, because you may need these key individuals to help you market your plan once it is complete. How do you go about networking? Here are some suggestions. Place a ☑ opposite those you can be enthusiastic about.

- ☐ Joining a trade or professional association in your career area. Attend meetings; make new friends; learn what is going on; decide where the career opportunities are.
- ☐ Attend conferences where you can meet other professionals in your area. Find out about any Plan B's they have.
- ☐ Attend formal classes, seminars or workshops and make new friends so you can exchange career information with them.
- ☐ Make the effort to create a mentor or two within your present organization.
- ☐ Start spending time with some Plan B enthusiasts in your (or other) organization.
- ☐ Contact professionals and arrange informational interviews to gain their suggestions on how to activate your Plan B when it is ready.

STRATEGY 1
BECOME A CAREER INFORMATION MAGNET

First you need to understand what is going on in the marketplace of your career specialty. What changes are taking place? What needs are not being filled? What new areas of expertise are employers seeking? What salary and benefit packages are being offered?

There are many ways to accumulate this kind of data. Check those below that have appeal.

- ☐ Become more active in trade associations. Attend meetings with networking in mind.
- ☐ Join other, related trade associations.
- ☐ Have lunch or after-work social meetings with knowledgeable people who are also information magnets.
- ☐ Subscribe to and study appropriate trade magazines.
- ☐ Attend trade conferences.
- ☐ Create a resource contact on your local campus.
- ☐ Share what you learn with others so they, in turn, will share with you.
- ☐ Do nice things for your ''network sources'' and enjoy doing it.
- ☐ Other: ____

  ____

  ____

The whole idea is to play the information game so that you are not left on the sidelines uninformed.

STRATEGY 2
REFINE AND EXPAND NETWORKING WITH INFORMATION INTERVIEWS

The more key people you can locate who are willing to discuss your career plans with you, or recommend you to others, the better. With a list of such people working for you you start to cover the market and your self-employment program moves into high gear. Not only does networking mean your calling on others, when you create good allies, they may call you. When your Plan B is nearing completion it is time to use networking to put the finishing touches to it. Those in your camp can help you refine it now and maintain it in the future. This can best be accomplished through information interviews.

An information interview is designed primarily to ''test the market'' on various issues such as competency standards, employment conditions, what employers are really seeking, etc. Although an information interview can be the first step finding a new opportunity, it is extremely valuable in its own right. Information interviews usually add fresh names to your networking system. There are also other advantages. Naturally, any information interview that leads to an *employment interview* falls into this category.

The key to gaining an information interview is your own attitude. If you are sincere in seeking information and communicate that you will be most appreciative should you receive it, chances are good the interview will be yours. Keep in mind that it is difficult for a person who has achieved status in a career field to turn down a newcomer when you ask for advice they are in a unique position to provide. Here are some tips.

- ☐ Seek people who are in key roles but not directly associated with employment. They receive fewer opportunities to help newcomers.
- ☐ Approach the interview with an open mind so you can discover new possibilities each time.
- ☐ Arrange to meet with them on their conditions (if appropriate offer to host them for lunch).
- ☐ Mention that you have a Plan B and would like advice regarding it.
- ☐ Listen carefully to all suggestions. Ask relevant questions.
- ☐ Ask who else might be in a position to provide you with insights and advice.
- ☐ Always send a thank you message.
- ☐ If appropriate, convert the beginning relationship into a mutually rewarding long-term one.
- ☐ Do not press beyond the individual's willingness to volunteer information and advice.

STRATEGY 3
EMPLOY AN "ENDLESS CHAIN" NETWORK SYSTEM

Regardless of the kind of networking you have done in the past, consider using an endless chain system. Below is a diagram. Start by listing two key people you feel would be receptive to looking at your Plan B, who are in a position to know of job openings in your specialty. Call each person and make a best effort to arrange a personal meeting. Mention you are completing your Plan B (this may intrigue them) and if you are successful in obtaining a meeting, take it with you.

Once in conversation, request additional names so that you can start your chain. Names provided should be people with whom the first party has an excellent relationship. Always ask if you can use the individual's name. With effort on your part, the endless chain networking system can live up to its name. You can keep it operational even after your Plan B turns into Plan A.

ENDLESS CHAIN NETWORKING

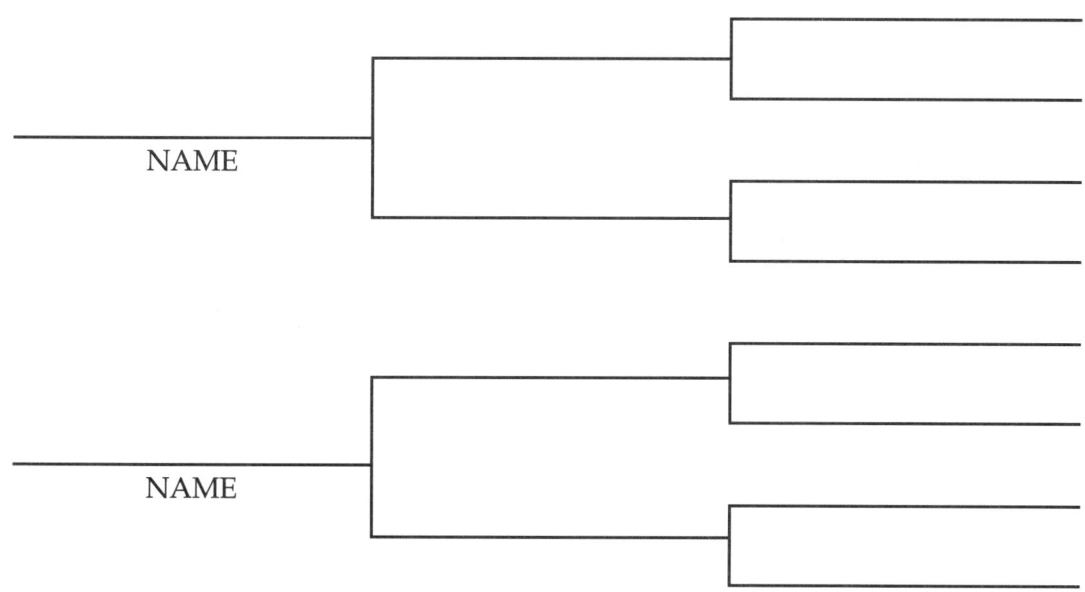

My personal goal is to add one new person to my networking system each

☐ day; ☐ week; ☐ month.

CASE 6: THE CONTACT THAT PAID OFF

Donna had been working undercover on her Plan B for over six months when her boss Mrs. MacCarthy came down hard on her over a mistake a co-worker made. At that moment, Donna decided to activate her Plan B.

The first person she decided to call was a Ms. Jamison, a human resource director for an electronics firm near her home. Donna met Ms. Jamison through a mutual friend, Hazel, at a conference on job burnout a few weeks earlier. Donna had to make four calls to reach Ms. Jamison (her secretary kept saying she was in a conference) but when the contact was made, Ms. Jamison was most receptive to an information interview and made an appointment for the following week.

The moment Ms. Jamison knew that Donna had almost completed her Plan B she showed immediate interest and they wound up having lunch together. Although Ms. Jamison's firm did not have an opening suitable for Donna, she knew of another firm who did and made arrangements for Donna to be interviewed by a Mr. Sledge.

Donna's qualifications (having been upgraded through her Plan B) were ideal and an employment offer was made, which Donna accepted with enthusiasm.

Donna's friend Hazel seemed bored and negative when she heard the story during lunch the following week. Hazel's comments: "You really lucked out, Donna. What happened to you seldom, if ever, happens to others. Frankly, I think networking of all kinds is overrated."

Do you agree with Hazel? Compare your thoughts with those of the author on page 86.

STEP 7
HAVE PLAN—WILL TRAVEL

This final step provides techniques on how to use your Plan B to win a better position either at your present firm or with another organization.

At this stage everything you know or have experienced about job hunting and employment interviews should be brought into play.

IF YOU HAVE DONE YOUR HOMEWORK, YOU WILL HAVE A SIGNIFICANT ADVANTAGE OVER OTHERS

Like a student graduating from college who has spent hours in placement offices preparing for his or her first serious job-hunting expedition, your Plan B has been prepared and you are ready. You have a Plan B to discuss with a superior inside of your organization or with a prospective employer outside. Study the suggestions below to learn how a Plan B can be used effectively.

SUGGESTION 1

INCLUDE A SUMMARY OF YOUR PLAN B IN YOUR RÉSUMÉ. In making a job change, past history is always important. You communicate this best with a creative résumé that incorporates information from your Plan B. A prospective employer may be more interested in your preparation for a new career than your previous experience or education. The best place to include your Plan B is at the very end of your résumé so you can highlight what you have done to upgrade yourself recently.

MARKETING YOUR PLAN B

SUGGESTION 2

INTRODUCE YOUR PLAN B DURING THE INTERVIEW PROCESS. Using good judgement, introduce your Plan B at the appropriate time. Explain why it was developed. Communicate how you have upgraded your skills. State how you think your Plan B prepared you to contribute more.

SUGGESTION 3

INVITE QUESTIONS ON YOUR PLAN. When a prospective employer becomes interested in your career development plan, you are doing well in the interview. Rather than being asked questions that may be difficult to answer, the interviewer is asking you questions that will allow you to demonstrate you are a creative person with initiative.

SUGGESTION 4

USE THE HOME FIELD ADVANTAGE. This means that through a Plan B you may now have, perhaps for the first time, an advantage with your present employer. Everything in your plan could help your present employer because you already know the ropes!

SUGGESTION 5

UNDERSTAND WHY YOUR PLAN B ENHANCES YOUR POTENTIAL. Anyone who completes a Plan B has demonstrated excellent potential to contribute to productivity because they have demonstrated they are proactive.

SUGGESTION 6

USE YOUR PLAN B IN A PROFESSIONAL MANNER. We earlier made the statement that when using a Plan B it is okay to play one end against the middle. In short, you can use your plan to gain the best possible position where you are now. If done openly and honestly, you can use an outside job offer as leverage to do this. Or, you can use a better "in-house" job offer as leverage to get a better position outside. This should be done without deception so neither party will wind up with bad feelings. Although there is nothing unethical or unprofessional in keeping a Plan B undercover during the preparation period, once you use it as a vehicle to gain a better position, the veil of secrecy should be lifted and it should be used with openness and pride.

Circle the suggestions made above that you intend to put into practice in the future: 1, 2, 3, 4, 5, 6.

PLEASE ANSWER THESE QUESTIONS

1. My general attitude toward developing a Plan B is:
   - Very enthusiastic ☐
   - Enthusiastic ☑
   - Lukewarm ☐
   - Negative ☐

2. My specific goal in doing a Plan B is to:
   - Improve my present job ☐
   - Get a new, better job ☐
   - Start a new career in a new field ☑
   - Get myself out of a rut ☑

3. My primary motivation in doing a Plan B is to:
   - Make more money ☐
   - Find a new identity ☑
   - Prove to myself that I can do it ☐
   - Be able to retire earlier ☐

INVITATION

APPENDIX II, PAGE 99 IS AN ADAPTATION OF THE SEVEN-STEP PLAN B STRATEGY FOR THOSE WHO ARE SEEKING A PART-TIME JOB DURING RETIREMENT. SOME RETIREES WISH TO WORK PART-TIME TO SUPPLEMENT THEIR RETIREMENT INCOME. OTHERS WANT A WORK INVOLVEMENT FOR SOCIAL OR PSYCHOLOGICAL REASONS. EITHER WAY, USING THE PLAN B APPROACH TO WIN THE RIGHT PART-TIME RETIREMENT JOB IS A SMART MOVE. NATURALLY, IT IS BEST TO GET STARTED BEFORE RETIREMENT STARTS.

P A R T

IV

MISCONCEPTIONS ABOUT HAVING A PLAN B

MYTHS ABOUT AN ALTERNATIVE GROWTH PROGRAM

A PLAN B WILL DISTRACT ME FROM PLAN A: Just the opposite is likely to happen! Looking outside your present career could give it more appeal, not less. Or you might see growth opportunities you have been neglecting. In any event, one plan can help the other. Once involved, you will discover you have time and energy for both.

DOING A PLAN B IS DISCOURAGING: Many individuals think that a Plan B is distasteful. They see it as reading want ads, lining up job prospects, and doing interviews. An alternative growth program is much more than a job-hunting expedition. In fact, developing a Plan B can be exciting for four reasons: (1) You can accomplish the plan while you have the security of a regular job. (2) It is a nonstressful way to lift yourself out of a situation that is leading nowhere. (3) It provides an opportunity to take a fresh look at your future (which is probably brighter than you suspect). (4) It can cause you to think at a higher level which, in some instances, can turn your life around.

A PLAN B IS TOO RISKY: This myth needs to be exploded quickly. Organizations recognize that employees should protect themselves from the winds of change. Upon learning that a productive employee is working on a Plan B, an enlightened manager should think: ''Perhaps we need to provide Julie with more opportunities here. If we can't, then I wish her luck elsewhere. She is entitled to her future.''

IT IS BETTER TO DO A PLAN B AS A FULL-TIME PROJECT: Some misguided individuals mistakenly believe it is better to start a growth program when they are unemployed. These people fail to recognize the security of having a Plan A (and the income that goes with it) makes it easier to design a superior plan. Outplacement counselors constantly describe the state many unemployed people fall into—a malaise that has a negative impact upon their ability to find a new position. A growth program, developed in advance, enables one to avoid this ''unemployment malaise.''

COMMON MISCONCEPTIONS

PLAN B MEANS MORE FORMAL EDUCATION: A career plan *may* require going back to school, but not always. What about those who already have the skills? Or those who want a similar job with another firm? Or those who want to improve their role through self-learning? Often a Plan B means taking advantage of Plan A learning opportunities now, so a move can be made later.

PLAN B IS FOR YOUNG AGGRESSIVE TYPES: Although a few ambitious young people may see the value of self-programming sooner, this does not mean they need it more. Just the opposite! Restructuring within a business often means the loss of upper- or mid-management jobs where salaries are higher and more fat can be cut. Also, those who have been around longer may have a greater psychological need to get out of a ''career rut.'' A Plan B offers the opportunity to break from the past and start over fresh.

PLAN B MEANS A GEOGRAPHICAL CHANGE: Rather than cause the uprooting of a family, a Plan B can keep you in your present home and location because of advance planning. When people lose their Plan A they often grasp at career straws that can turn their lifestyle upside down. A well-designed growth program can help a person through a major career change with a minimum of disruption. Properly perceived, a Plan B can play a major role in helping you be true to your future.

HUBIE

Hubie graduated from the business program of Ohio State University as a computer programmer. He was encouraged by his professors to join a major company as a trainee and work his way up the management ladder. After years of hard work with uneven progress, Hubie began to challenge the wisdom of his decision. Why should he confine his talents to one firm? Why should he wait to be promoted from within? Why should he hitch his future to a single corporation?

Unexpectedly, Hubie's company merged with a competitor. His job was taken by a person from the other company. Despite all of his educational preparation, productivity and creative contributions to his company, Hubie was left out in the cold.

Why hadn't he been taught to program his own career so he could protect his future?

WHY SO MANY INDIVIDUALS NEVER DEVELOP A PLAN B

Shocking as it may seem, it is estimated that less than 10 out of every 100 workers have a well-developed alternative career plan. Reasons for this situation of "nonreadiness" are many. Three of the most obvious, and understandable, are:

1. Higher education places so much emphasis on preparing students to succeed in a Plan A they neglect to point out the need for a backup program. The rationale is that you must have a successful Plan A before you are ready for a Plan B and it is not logical to do both at the same time. "Win your first career opportunity and after you have settled in, you can worry about a Plan B. First things first."

2. Many people feel there is something unethical about preparing a Plan B while on a firm's payroll. They feel it shows a lack of loyalty or honesty. On top of this, some feel building a Plan B will place their Plan A in jeopardy. If your boss discovers you are working on an alternative career possibility, she or he may take a dim view. You may have rendered yourself ineligible for promotions or fair treatment in the future. In case of a reduction, you may be the first to go. Many individuals have yet to discover the mutual advantages of developing career alternatives.

3. Perhaps the biggest reason for not developing alternative plans is that most individuals are not motivated to prepare one. It is all they can do to keep a Plan A and their home life going. They can tread water but nothing more. "Don't talk to me about something better when I am barely hanging on to what I have." These individuals need to be convinced that having a Plan B will make their Plan A more comfortable while also improving their lifestyle.

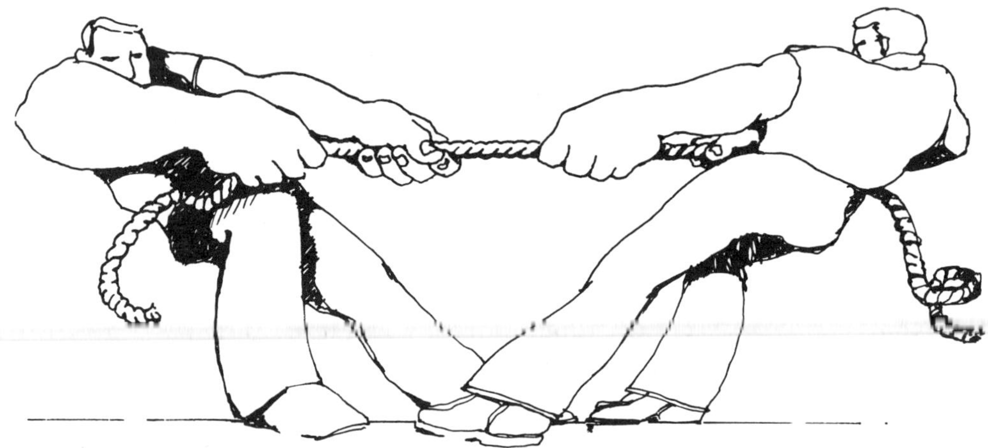

WHEN IT COMES TO A PLAN A AND B, IT IS OKAY TO PLAY BOTH ENDS AGAINST THE MIDDLE *

* Providing, of course, you continue to be effective in your Plan A.

HOW WILL OTHERS REACT?

When Jessica called her sister Kim to explain how her strategy got her a higher paying, more creative position Kim replied: "Great. When we meet next week I want to know all of the details so I can do one of my own."

When Cody made the decision to activate his Plan B he told the whole story to his boss who replied: "With all of the changes going on around here you did the right thing. It may come as a surprise but I am in the process of doing one of my own."

When Dawn received a big promotion she decided to stay with her Plan A but continue to maintain her Plan B. In talking to her boss about her previously secret plan, he replied: "I am complimented that you would discuss your plan with me and I can see now it had a lot to do with your receiving the promotion. I just hope we can continue to provide you with sufficient challenge to keep you working with us."

PRE-TEST

There are many opinions and a few misconceptions about whether a Plan B should be kept secret or communicated to co-workers or superiors. This exercise will help you make your decision. When finished, compare your answers with those below.

True	False	
_____	_____	1. Most people are more motivated to reach a secret goal.
_____	_____	2. There is nothing unethical in preparing a Plan B in secret.
_____	_____	3. Discussing a Plan B prematurely with co-workers can get it into the grapevine and be counterproductive.
_____	_____	4. The development of a Plan B can cause one to stay with Plan A.
_____	_____	5. This book recommends that the reader design, complete, and activate a Plan B while remaining effective with Plan A.
_____	_____	6. Today, most management people are less approving of employees with a Plan B.
_____	_____	7. A Plan B can cause you to contribute more to an organization.
_____	_____	8. Most people do not take it seriously when they hear someone is preparing a Plan B.
_____	_____	9. You and you alone are responsible for your career future.
_____	_____	10. The time will never arrive when organizations conduct Plan B seminars for their employees.

ANSWERS: 1. F (there is no evidence either way on this) 2. T (one has the right to prepare a Plan B and it is not unethical as long as she or he remains effective with Plan A) 3. T (one should be selective in sharing plans on the development of a Plan B) 4. T (this is one reason why enlightened managers are often in favor of employees preparing a Plan B) 5. T (whether one communicates it to superiors is a personal decision) 6. F (the ''winds of change'' have caused management to be more approving) 7. T (the reason this is true will be explained later) 8. T (this occurs because people talk about back-up plans but few actually develop one) 9. T (and you are free to make a change at any time) 10. F (a few organizations conduct serious career development programs now)

THE INTRIGUE OF SECRECY

There is nothing unethical about preparing a Plan B while you continue to operate effectively in the job you were hired to perform. For several reasons, however, some individuals prefer to keep their career contingency planning undercover. They do not discuss it with co-workers or superiors. Reasons why secrecy is preferred by some individuals, include:

> ''The moment I started working on a Plan B my regular job became easier and more fun. My new attitude was noticed by co-workers. A few thought I had a secret lover. Believe me, I enjoyed the mystique my secrecy created.''
>
> ''I think one is motivated to do a better job with a Plan B when you keep your efforts secret. Knowing you are developing something that you can fall back on frees you to see things differently. You feel proud that you have the guts to do it. It is a little like being the cat that swallowed the canary.''
>
> ''It was nobody's fault, but when I realized I was boxed in with my Plan A, I started a Plan B. My attitude improved immediately. It was then I decided to keep it secret. I didn't want to jepordize my Plan A and was successful because I recently received a promotion.''

Whether you complete your Plan B with or without communication at your Plan A workstation is a personal choice. Every individual and situation is different. The approach that motivates you the most is the one recommended.

''Our plans miscarry because they have no aim. When a man does not know what harbor he is making for, no wind is the right wind.''

Seneca (4 B.C.-A.D. 65)

PART

V

LAUNCHING YOUR PLAN

"Man has a limited biological capacity to change. When this capacity is overwhelmed, the capacity is in future shock."

Alvin Toffler

HAVE A PENCIL IN HAND AS YOU CONSIDER THESE SUGGESTIONS

SUGGESTION 1

First read through the MODEL on the next two pages. Although Sara Cottonwood's situation and background may not be similar to yours, you may get some ideas. You are encouraged to follow this format.

SUGGESTION 2

Start your plan now. Understand you will need to do some research later to complete it but just getting started is a big step!

SUGGESTION 3

Consult with those who constitute your support group (or others) as you proceed. View your Plan B as a major project. Six months or more may be required to complete it.

SUGGESTION 4

Be true to yourself. The MODEL was designed to provide guidance in the preparation of your own special plan. Yours could be far more sophisticated and demanding.

A MODEL TO GUIDE YOU

Sara Cottonwood
Graduate: Central Arkansas State University
Major: Business Administration

Special competencies: Office management and computer skills. Currently employed as office supervisor for Southern Supply Co., Inc.

My overall goal is to win a more promising management position in a larger, more progressive firm that has excellent benefits, higher salaries, and more upward mobility.

STEP 1: COMMIT YOURSELF

I selected option 5 because my close friend and co-worker Margaret and I will work together. We plan to have dinner together every Tuesday after work and share the progress we are making.

STEP 2: DO BETTER AT YOUR PRESENT JOB

I checked eight of the streamlining suggestions and will follow through on them in the next few weeks. In addition, I intend to do the following:

- Delegate more to others in my office.
- Make a list of daily priorities so that I have a minimum of 30 minutes each noon hour to work on my Plan B.
- Ask my superior to assign my credit union responsibilities to another manager.
- Demonstrate more leadership so others will not flood me with work they should be doing themselves.

STEP 3: LEARN MORE FROM WHERE YOU ARE

I have isolated the following three learning opportunities where I work and will pursue them when time permits and the situation is right.

- Negotiation Strategies Workshop March 6th & 7th
- Leadership Seminar April 16th
- Word Processing Software, learn via company tutorial

SARA COTTONWOOD'S PLAN B

STEP 4:
IMPROVE YOUR PRESENT SKILLS

Here are the competency standards that I intend to reach during the next six months.

- Upgrade computer application skills in the area of word processing and database management
- Improve my communication and counseling skills

STEP 5:
BACK TO SCHOOL? SELF-INSTRUCTION? BOTH?

Each semester until my Plan B is complete I will enroll at the university for courses in database management. Successful completion of these courses will make me
proficient in the latest generation of relational databases.

I recognize that I need to improve my management skills. I will do this both by attending company seminars and at night on a self-paced basis. I will subscribe to *Office Management*

STEP 6:
CREATIVE NETWORKING: GET STARTED TODAY

I plan to build my network on an ongoing basis. I intend to add one person per week to a list composed of key individuals. Each will be in a position to give me both guidance and contacts. I anticipate at least 50 percent of these key people will come from my trade group. To improve my accessibility to such people I intend to become an officer in that association. I now have three people on my list. I hope to wind up with 15.

STEP 7:
HAVE PLAN— WILL TRAVEL

Although I may change my mind when the time arrives, I plan to activate my Plan B when it is finished. I like the challenge of doing this while I continue to make progress with my present firm. My goal is to increase my annual income by $10,000 or more (with comparable benefits). When the time is right, I will speed up my networking and use my Plan B for both information and actual job interviews. Frankly, I am more excited about my future than at any time since I graduated from college seven years ago. Margaret feels the same way.

Wish me luck!

PLAN B WORKSHEETS

Your name: ____

Anticipated date of completion: ____________________________

Overall goal I wish to accomplish. Please write it out.

____

____

STEP 1
COMMIT YOURSELF

I am going with Option #_____. My reasons are:

____

____

STEP 2
DO BETTER AT YOUR PRESENT JOB

To free myself to develop my Plan B, I intend to streamline my present job in the following ways:

____

____

____

STEP 3
LEARN MORE FROM WHERE YOU ARE

I have isolated the following learning opportunities where I work:

____

____

____

WORKSHEETS (continued)

STEP 4
IMPROVE YOUR PRESENT SKILLS

Here are the competency standards that I intend to reach:

____

____

____

STEP 5
BACK TO SCHOOL? SELF-INSTRUCTION? BOTH?

I will enroll in and complete the following courses:

____

____

____

My self-help learning program at home will include:

____

____

____

STEP 6
CREATIVE NETWORKING: GET STARTED TODAY

My networking strategy will be: (I will or will not use the endless chain networking system.)

____

____

____

STEP 7
HAVE PLAN— WILL TRAVEL

Whether or not I activate my Plan B when completed will depend upon:

____

____

____

WHEN DOUBTS REMAIN

It is natural for some readers to remain skeptical about the Plan B concept. Is it really worth all of the time and effort? Would there really be a substantial payoff for me?

Obviously, you must find agreement within yourself on the value of a Plan B. To help you do this, three hypothetical cases are presented. Please read, react and then compare your views with those of the author.

CASE 8: JEREMY & PAUL

Jeremy and Paul's relationship was work oriented. They have been in the same department, doing the same basic work for four years. Although both are the same age, have similar backgrounds and are married with children, they did not see each other socially.

Last year rumors persisted that their firm would go through a major restructuring and some departments would be eliminated. Jeremy took the rumors seriously and encouraged Paul to do the same. In fact, he suggested they help each other develop a Plan B. Paul showed no interest, so Jeremy independently started work on one. Among other things, it included going back to school to upgrade his skills and the beginnings of a job search.

When the announcement was made that their department had been eliminated, Paul was in a state of shock. He asked Jeremy to have a beer with him that afternoon. "Jer," said Paul, "I'm really scared about the future. In addition to our mortgage, we owe on our cars and have other bills. I guess we should have taken those rumors seriously." Jeremy replied: "I did, Paul, but you will recall you were not interested at the time. Let me tell you what I have been doing and perhaps it will help you get started."

Is it too late for Paul to do a Plan B? Please write out your answer in the spaces provided and turn to page 86 to compare your views.

____

____

____

____

____

CASE 9: GERRY

Gerry, newly employed by Trac Corporation, was discouraged by the complacency of her more experienced co-workers. Sensing that her future was limited at Trac, she started work on a Plan B. A major part of her strategy was to take advantage of her present job by learning more. She asked to learn how to operate the latest equipment. She asked for more responsibility when new programs were introduced. This helped provide more knowledge and contributed to her positive attitude. Gerry kept her personal productivity high, not to impress her superiors, but to prepare herself for another career opportunity.

One morning, to her surprise, Gerry was invited into the division manager's office and offered the position of department manager. The new position would give her a 20 percent increase in salary and new opportunities to learn.

Is this case realistic? Is it possible that in preparing for a better job elsewhere an employee can receive an unusual opportunity at home? Please express your views and compare with those of the author on page 86.

____

____

____

____

____

CASE 10: LARRY

Almost everyone around the plant knew about the conflict between Larry and his boss. Unfortunately, it was so hard on Larry that he required professional help. Things started to get better only after the counselor suggested that Larry start making plans to free himself from a situation that was untenable for both him and his family.

It came as no surprise when Larry resigned. What did surprise everyone was hearing that Larry had developed a Plan B and had an offer to join a competitive organization with a superior position. In discussing the situation later with a former colleague, Larry said: "It was obvious months ago that I could not build a good relationship, so I took the only door open to me. I kept learning and protecting myself while I did some upgrading and serious networking. Do I have hard feelings? Just the opposite. Without the problem I would not have been motivated to do a Plan B in the first place."

What was the real advantage of a Plan B to Larry? Please write out your answer and compare with that found on page 86.

____

____

____

____

____

MAINTENANCE IDEAS!

We earlier compared a Plan B to an insurance policy or having money wisely invested. When it comes to maintaining a completed Plan B it might be best to compare it to a fine automobile. Just like any mechanical device, a plan can deteriorate and become inoperative if not used properly or neglected.

To maintain an automobile you must put in gas and oil, get an occasional lube job and keep the engine tuned. Now and then some repairs will be necessary. To maintain a Plan B you must keep your skills at high standards, continue your networking efforts, schedule information interviews on a regular basis, and review and revise your Plan B as required. Your Plan B shouldn't gather cobwebs.

Listed below are some Plan B maintenance tips. Please place a ☑ opposite those you intend to honor.

☐ Keep your plan and this book in a prominent place as a reminder that you have the equivalent of a career insurance policy (providing you keep your Plan B up-to-date).

☐ Thumb through your plan every three months to see if deletions or additions need to be made.

☐ Remind yourself that your plan is, in effect, your mental health protection plan. It provides you with both freedom and security.

☐ Your plan should pay you interest. That is, it should provide you with psychological dividends like increased motivation, confidence, and a greater willingness to take risks.

☐ One of the best ways to maintain a Plan B is to help someone else do one. In doing this, you may discover a weakness in your own.

☐ An ideal time to do a ''maintenance check'' is when you return from a professional meeting or trade conference. New trends, competency standards and additions to your network should be added.

COMMON MISTAKES

Four common mistakes are listed below. Now that you have almost finished this book, which one are you most apt to make? Place a ☑ in the appropriate box.

☐ **UNDERESTIMATING THE EXCITEMENT AND INTRIGUE INVOLVED.** Many people consider developing and maintaining a Plan B as work. They are wrong. Like taking a first trip in a balloon, a well-developed plan can provide a new perspective on your career and future. This happens because you free yourself from organizational dependency. It's a greet feeling!

☐ **FIGURING YOU HAVE A PLAN WHEN YOU DON'T.** Now that you know what is involved (seven steps) you might not make this mistake. Still, you might be tempted to take too many shortcuts. You do not want to pay premiums on an insurance policy that you can't collect on when the chips are down.

☐ **WAITING TOO LONG TO GET STARTED.** If you were to receive notice today that your job will be eliminated in 30 days you waited too long. Few good plans can be prepared and completed in less than three months.

☐ **REFUSING TO SEE THE FULL VALUE.** Some people persist in thinking that a Plan B does little more than win you a promotion or another job. In addition, a true plan can enhance your Plan A, contribute to fulfilling your life goals and provide you with a new, exciting philosophy of work.

SELF-QUIZ

Please answer the following true-false questions.

TRUE	FALSE	
	✓	1. You can't have a Plan B without a Plan A.
✓		2. The value of a Plan B does not depend upon whether or not it is exercised.
	✓	3. Having a secret Plan B is unethical.
	✓	4. A Plan B will provide you with the career you should have chosen years ago.
✓		5. The further you fall behind in job skills of your specialty the longer it will take you to complete a Plan B.
✓		6. Networking is building strong, mutually rewarding relationships with people who are in a position to help you activate your Plan B when it is ready.
✓		7. An information interview is designed to keep you in touch with the job market and those competencies required.
	✓	8. Networking and information interviews are a minor part of developing a Plan B.
✓		9. A Plan B frequently sends the preparer back to college.
✓		10. Some individuals improve their skills through assuming more responsibility in their current job.

SELF-QUIZ (continued)

TRUE	FALSE	
✓		11. Self-learning at home can sometimes contribute as much to a successful Plan B as formal learning on campus.
	✓	12. A good time to construct a Plan B is while you are drawing unemployment insurance.
	✓	13. The moment your Plan B is operational it becomes your Plan A and you need another Plan B.
✓		14. The best way to make yourself more marketable is to improve your job skills.
✓		15. The three best ways to improve your special competencies are to: (1) learn more at your present job (2) take college courses (3) engage in self-learning at home.
	✓	16. Once a Plan B is complete it does not require maintenance for at least a year.
✓		17. A Plan B is essentially a philosophy toward work.
✓		18. Many colleges now offer seminars on the significance of having a Plan B and how to develop one.
✓		19. Lack of motivation is the number one reason most people do not have a Plan B.
	✓	20. Restructuring, mergers and relocations are a passing fad and will slow down in the future.

TRUE	FALSE	
✓		21. It is estimated that less than 10 percent of those employed full-time have a workable Plan B.
	✓	22. The program presented in this book contains a seven-step process that can be completed in a few weeks.
	✓	23. Doing a Plan B is all work and no play.
	✓	24. The endless chain system is an interviewing technique.
✓		25. A Plan B is designed to improve your Plan A while it prepares you to lose it.

EACH CORRECT ANSWER IS WORTH FOUR POINTS.

TOTAL SCORE 88

3 wrong

(Correct answers on the following page.)

ANSWERS TO SELF-QUIZ

COMPARE YOUR ANSWERS WITH THOSE OF THE AUTHOR:

1. TRUE — A Plan A is your present career role, a Plan B is an alternative yet to be exercised.
2. TRUE — Sometimes developing a Plan B motivates one to do a better job with Plan A and a promotion makes it undesirable to move.
3. FALSE — There is nothing unethical about protecting your future from the modern winds of change.
4. FALSE — Finding the right career is a separate matter. A Plan B, however, can lead you in the right direction.
5. TRUE — When you fall too far behind, going back to college may be necessary and this takes time.
6. TRUE — Advance networking is a critical part of any Plan B.
7. TRUE — This is necessary so you will know when your Plan B is complete and operational.
8. FALSE — A major part!
9. TRUE — Taking a college course (or earning a degree) is often the only way to reach one's Plan B goals.
10. TRUE — These are very perceptive and smart individuals.
11. TRUE — Self-learning at home is on the increase. More publications are available.
12. FALSE — You can't do a Plan B without a Plan A.
13. TRUE — This means you may develop more than one Plan B.
14. TRUE — In most fields, skill improvement (retraining) is increasingly necessary.
15. TRUE — Steps 5, 6, and 7 in the Plan B process.
16. FALSE — Like maintaining an automobile, frequent repairs and tuning are required.
17. TRUE — A Plan B has both a pragmatic and philosophical side.
18. FALSE — Hopefully they may do so in the future.
19. TRUE — Most people talk Plan B but actually do little in constructing one.
20. FALSE — Most experts believe the trend will continue for at least ten years—perhaps into the next century.
21. TRUE — The author believes this low percentage figure will increase substantially in the next few years.
22. FALSE — Seven steps, yes; but there is too much involved to complete a good plan in a few weeks.
23. FALSE — Doing a plan can and should also be fun.
24. FALSE — The endless chain system is a networking technique.
25. TRUE — This is a paradox some find difficult to accept.

AUTHOR'S SUGGESTED ANSWERS TO CASES

CASE 1: RICHARD

If both Richard and his wife Marie are giving consideration to the Uncle George possibility, it seems that Marie questions her ability to provide enough motivation. If Uncle George is the best model Richard has available, and if Uncle George is willing to go with an informal contract, the author feels this might be the best motivator. This arrangement would be less complex to start with and easier for Richard to maintain. Although Richard can communicate his plan to the other people (and they can be of help along the way) his commitment to Uncle George could provide 90 percent of the motivation required.

CASE 2: CONFLICT

James does not see the long-range, true value of a Plan B. He refuses to see that he can make changes now that will help him no matter what happens in the future. James subscribes to the old-fashioned theory that the only way to get a better job is to dump your present one first. Gregg believes you can use a present job, no matter how unpleasant it may be, to gain a better one.

CASE 3: ATTITUDE REVERSAL

It is doubtful that Tanya will be able to turn things around in her present job. Because of this, it might be best for her not to expect so much from herself but rather do other things to prepare a Plan B. Although it is best to make all possible improvements with Plan A while working on Plan B, all of the major behavioral reverses she must make are not realistic.

CASE 4: JACK'S PROBLEM

It depends just how much improvement Jack must make to bring his skills up to standard. If the gap is extremely wide, it might be best for him to return to campus full time. Once caught up, Jack can try for a fresh start. If, however, the gap is modest, Jack's three-step approach can work and will produce less strain on himself.

AUTHOR'S SUGGESTED ANSWERS TO CASES (continued)

CASE 5: CHALLENGE FOR MARY

Mary is lucky that she has such a good opportunity to carve out a practical career for herself. She should find out, however, how long it would be before she could be transferred into the marketing department. The combination of college work, self-study, and on-the-job learning is ideal. With Mary's background, progress should be speedy.

CASE 6: THE CONTACT THAT PAID OFF

Hazel is expressing a sour grapes attitude because she has never given networking a chance. True, networking can lead one up blind alleys, but it takes only one right contact to wind up a winner. Donna is to be congratulated for being so persistant.

CASE 7: PLAN B SEMINARS

The author is of the opinion that any large organization, especially one that is downsizing, would benefit from offering employees such a seminar. There would be some exceptions, but generally speaking, helping people develop a Plan B would increase productivity and encourage them to remain rather than leave.

CASE 8: JEREMY & PAUL

It is not too late for Paul to get started on finding a new job but it is too late for him to prepare a Plan B. The reader is reminded that a Plan B is developed ahead of time while the individual still has a Plan A. Jeremy stands a chance of finding a better job. Paul may have to initially settle for something beneath his previous responsibilities.

CASE 9: GERRY

The author contends that this case is highly realistic because Gerry's Plan B caused her to live up to her potential while the other employees drifted along. Thus, her performance stood out. It was not important for management to know she has a Plan B.

CASE 10: LARRY

When Larry started to develop a departure plan, he kept himself from being victimized. Without a plan, Larry could have become so bitter and frustrated that he would have been damaged. A Plan B can help one do a better job of surviving until a new opportunity opens up. Sometimes a Plan B is the only way to turn a bad situation into an excellent one.

APPENDIX I

RATE YOUR CURRENT JOB-GETTING SKILLS

ATTITUDE

PROSPECTING

NETWORKING

TELEPHONE SKILLS

RESUME PREPARATION

INTERVIEW PREPARATION

INTERVIEW TECHNIQUES

IMAGE AND GROOMING

SKILL UPGRADING

UTILIZING SUPPORT SERVICES

CREATING YOUR OWN JOB

GOALS: SELF-DISCIPLINE

INTRODUCTION

This exercise is designed to provide you with special insights regarding your techniques and strategies as a job-finder and job-winner. Once you discover your strengths and weaknesses you will be in a better position to start your search. Almost everyone can benefit.

- If you feel secure but unhappy in your present position and seek a different, more enjoyable one, you will learn about the 12 steps involved in making such a move.
- If you anticipate being thrown into the labor market in the near future, you can isolate weaknesses ahead of time, make corrections and be better prepared should the time come.
- If you are already unemployed, this exercise will assist you in reviewing your present strategy and make immediate improvements.
- If you will soon graduate from college and you need to prepare for your first interviews.
- If you are still in school and seek a part-time job.
- If you will soon retire and want to work part-time to keep involved and supplement your income.

There are two sections to the exercise. First, you rate yourself in the 12 categories that are normally a part of the job-seeking process. Second, you construct a VISUAL PROFILE that will point out your current strengths and weaknesses.

This exercise will give you the professional approach you need to succeed.

Good luck!

RATING YOURSELF IN TWELVE CATEGORIES

You will now rate yourself in 12 selected areas on what you feel to be your present state of knowledge, experience and effectiveness. Please read the material and then make the most honest evaluation possible. You do this when you circle the appropriate number from 1 to 10.

- If you circle the number 1, 2 or 3, you are saying you have limited knowledge and experience in this area and need substantial help.
- If you circle the number 4, 5, 6 or 7, you are telling yourself that considerable improvement is needed.
- If you circle an 8, 9 or 10, you are giving yourself a signal you need only a little improvement in this category.

Please be as honest with yourself as possible. Keep in mind that most people rate themselves high in a few areas and low in a few others. Take your time, as it will be from these ratings that you will build your profile and plan your strategy.

1. ATTITUDE

As Tom Jackson, author of *Guerilla Tactics in the Job Market* has well-observed, the job-hunting process may best be described as NO NO NO NO NO NO NO NO NO NO NO NO NO NO NO NO NO NO NO NO NO NO NO NO NO NO NO NO NO NO NO NO NO NO YES. Hearing a few no's and getting a few rejections is usually a part of job-finding. What is your attitude toward this aspect of the job-search process? Can you take rejections and bounce back?

What about your ability to transmit a positive work attitude during interviews? Does your voice say you are anxious to contribute while your attitude says you are not?

Can you interpret the entire job-search process as a ''game'' or do you hate the prospects before you get started?

If you have a highly positive attitude toward conducting a professional job search, give yourself 2 points. If you are positive about using every possible resource to set up interviews, give yourself another 2 points. If you are willing to upgrade your skills *as you search for a job* give yourself 2 additional points. If you think you can maintain a positive attitude over a long stretch of time, increase your total to 9 or 10 points.

RATING YOURSELF (continued)

Keep in mind that in any job search, a positive attitude can be your most priceless possession. It is your most valuable personality characteristic. Please rate yourself as high as you can realistically justify.

Low									High
1	2	3	4	5	6	7	8	9	10

2. PROSPECTING

An employer is qualified as a true prospect when he has an opening for which you qualify and is willing to give you an interview. *Prospecting is how you find such employers.* You see unemployed people checking want ads in newspapers and trade journals, visiting placement agencies and many other prospecting techniques.

Each job search requires a tailored prospecting system. Such a system involves extensive research to identify organizations who could utilize your skills and targeting those for whom you would like to work. Some prospecting ideas can be gained from reading books or interviewing those who found jobs in your area ahead of you. Other prospecting techniques will come from experience.

In most situations, people spend more time finding prospects than they do preparing for and going through interviews. One reason for this is that 25 percent of all jobs are with smaller firms that are more difficult to find. A good system reaches deeply into all segments of the employment market—including all government agencies.

If you have already designed a system that produces two or more qualified prospects per week, give yourself a high grade. If you are confident (through experience) that you can develop such a system, give yourself a score between a 4 and 6. If you have apprehensions about your skill in finding prospects, give yourself a 3 or under.

Low									High
1	2	3	4	5	6	7	8	9	10

3. NETWORKING

Networking is building a series of strong relationships with people who are in a key position to help you find and win a position where you could reach your potential. Networking can create a chain of events that will lead you to qualified prospects. The players in any system are key people who are in a position to know others who might be interested in your services. Often they are respected people already well known in your specific field (college professors, consultants, directors of human resource departments). The best way to meet new people who can become part of your networking chain is to join a trade group and attend meetings.

In contacting such people, it is important that you do not communicate you are desperate to get a job, but, rather, you would like suggestions and advice. It is also vital that any relationship created be mutually rewarding—that is, anyone who helps you should enjoy the satisfaction of being a mentor.

Getting the right job is more a matter of good networking than luck. It is *through* networking that you are more apt to wind up at the right place at the right time.

Give yourself a high grade only if you understand the full implications of networking and already have a system in operation. Give yourself an average score if you see the possibilities in networking and have the confidence to initiate a system starting today. If you don't understand networking and it leaves you frustrated, give yourself a low score.

4. TELEPHONE SKILLS

The telephone is the serious job hunter's best friend. Not only can it help you find prospects, the telephone can help you get interview appointments. Used effectively, it can make your job search easier and more effective.

Telemarketing yourself involves such techniques as developing your best voice, accepting rebuffs without getting discouraged, being extra pleasant to switchboard operators, receptionists and secretaries so you can *get through* to the key people, presenting yourself in such a way that people want to give you an interview and being persistant.

People who are afraid to make skillfull use of the telephone in their job search should circle a low number; those who have confidence to use the telephone but have yet to learn telemarketing techniques should circle a middle number; those who already consider themselves telemarketing experts and are anxious to market themselves should circle a high number.

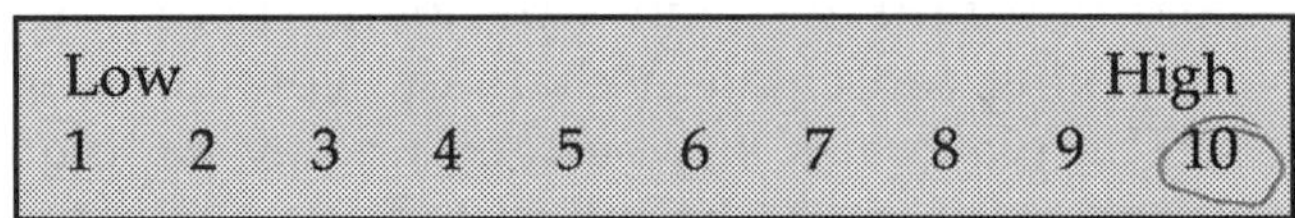

5. RÉSUMÉ PREPARATION

A résumé is usually a one or two page history of your achievements, education and characteristics that qualify you for the position you seek. Résumés are designed primarily to gain interviews but they have many additional uses. Experts claim a résumé should be tailored to the specific job under consideration. Are you already an expert at résumé preparation or should you find a book on the subject or work with a professional?

And don't forget the right cover letter should accompany your résumé. Models can usually be found in books that deal with résumé preparation.

If you recognize you are weak in this area and need a professional to help you prepare and edit a resume that will produce interviews, give yourself a 3 or under; if you can do one following instructions in a book, give yourself a 6 or under; if you have recently prepared a résumé that has produced excellent results, give yourself a higher grade.

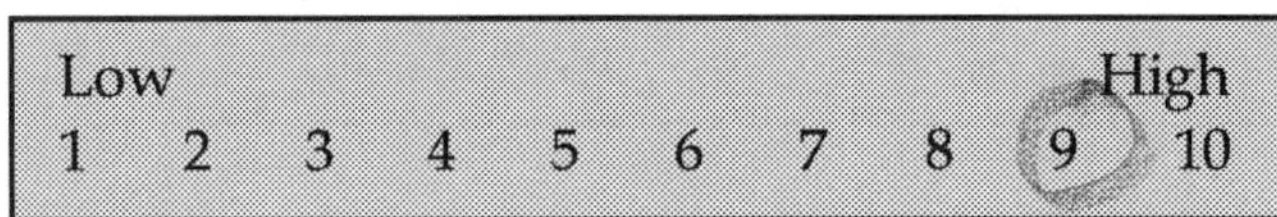

6. INTERVIEW PREPARATION

All 12 steps within the job-winning process are important. The face-to-face interview is critical. How you prepare for it can be as important as the way you perform once it happens. Are you following an exercise program so you appear healthy, eager and willing to contribute to the productivity level expected by your future employer? Once you get an interview appointment, do you research the background of the firm in preparation for the questioning that usually takes place? Can you answer questions like: What do you know about us? Why did you select us over other firms? Can you name the president of our company? Why did you leave your last employer? What is your career objective? What are your weaknesses? What are your salary expectations? Keep in mind that few employers are interested in "wishy-washy" applicants who cannot provide decisive answers.

Rate yourself on the state of readiness you anticipate you will be in when interviews take place. Will you really have done your homework?

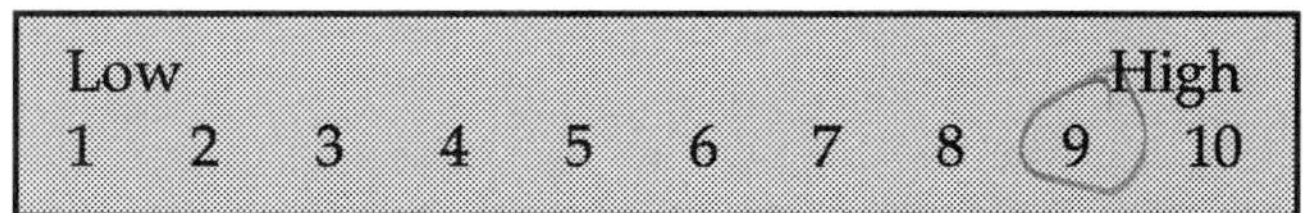

7. INTERVIEW TECHNIQUES

There are a number of techniques that need to be mastered if one wishes an employment interview to turn out successfully. Keeping eye contact when answering questions, injecting humor when the situation calls for it and asking questions of your own are all recommended. The overriding technique is to *be yourself;* transmit a willingness to learn; be flexible; and adapt to the new environment. On many college campuses these days, students are encouraged to do hypothetical interviews that can be rated by other students and the instructor. Assume that you prepared for a hypothetical interview and put it on video. Now sit back and rate yourself. Use the scale below to indicate how you *think* you would rate yourself.

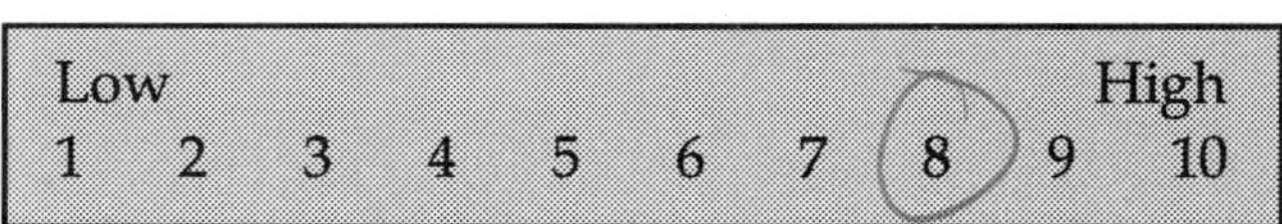

8. IMAGE AND GROOMING

What kind of a first impression would you make under the stress of a job interview? Would you be wearing clothes appropriate for the position for which you are applying? For example, a conservative dress or suit might communicate the best image when being interviewed for a position with a financial institution, where something more flamboyant would be appropriate when applying for a position with a media organization. Neatness, cleanliness, use of cosmetics and hairstyle all contribute to the image communicated.

Employers are prohibited from taking race, sex, age, and physical disabilities into consideration, but what you wear and how you have prepared yourself can influence whether you are accepted or rejected. Please circle where you think you would fall in this sensitive area.

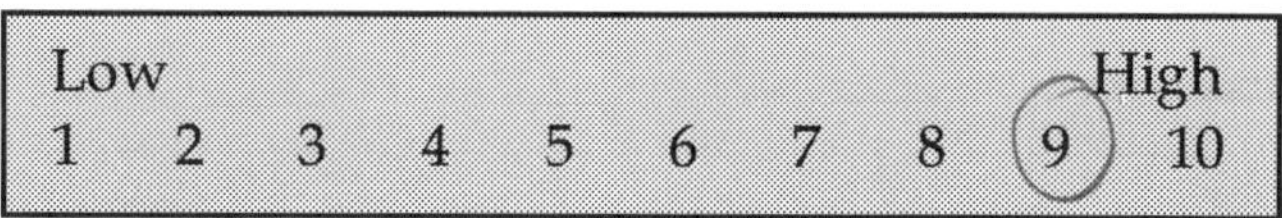

9. SKILL UPGRADING

Employers often require specific skill or competency performance in certain positions. Aptitudes, talents and personality characteristics often play an important role. In some areas, for example clerical and mechanical, proof of performance levels is often requested. Today, because of technological advancements and continuous upgrading, skills need to be maintained and improved to stay competitive in the labor market.

If you feel you are *fully* competent in all of the skills required in the position for which you are applying, give yourself a high score. If you feel you are *moderately* prepared, rate yourself somewhere in the middle. If you are seeking a job knowing your skills are inferior, give yourself a low grade and do something to improve them immediately.

Low									High
1	2	3	4	5	6	7	8	9	10

10. UTILIZING SUPPORT SERVICES

Both prospecting and networking involve making the maximum use of all available support services. Colleges provide outstanding support services to their students both before and after graduation—yet some students do not take advantage of the help they can provide. The same is true with private employment agencies and government operated human resource departments. In some communities it is possible to join a self-help Job Club where a small group of people meet every week or so to provide suggestions and encouragement to each other. Retraining should also be viewed as a support group. Yet, some unemployed people do not make the most of such opportunities.

What is your attitude toward searching out and taking full advantage of all the help available to you? If you are willing to accept other people and available agencies as partners in your search, give yourself a high score. If you prefer to go it alone, perhaps feeling you are "above" seeking help from others, give yourself a much lower score. Many people permit personal pride to keep them from accepting the kind of guidance and help they need.

Low									High
1	2	3	4	5	6	7	8	9	10

11. CREATING YOUR OWN JOB

Sometimes, after exploring all available possibilities to get on a payroll with all the benefits, individuals decide to set up their own positions in their own homes. Some contract to do work (free-lance artists); others build a clientele for special services (consultants); still others set up a small business (landscaping, auto repair, etc.) with only a minimum of overhead expenses. Many people are anxious and willing to take an off-beat, part-time job to hold them over financially until they can get a small operation of their own started. Have you fully investigated such possibilities? Do you have entrepreneurial instincts? Do you have a profession or special talent that lends itself to your operating as an individual?

If you think your résumé communicates the possibilities of independent work and *you are highly motivated in this direction,* demonstrate your interest by giving yourself a high score. If, however, you have no interest in this category, give yourself a score of 1.

Low									High
1	2	3	4	5	6	7	8	9	10

12. GOALS: SELF-DISCIPLINE

Goal-oriented people usually find it easier to win a new job than others. In fact, those who consistently set and reach personal goals are seldom out of work in the first place. Why? Because they usually have a Plan B ready to put into operation the moment their Plan A job loses luster or disappears. They do not wait until they are unemployed to test their marketability and they view networking as an insurance policy against unemployment.

Successful job seekers should set goals for themselves at three levels. Level one: The number of interviews they seek each week. Level two: The review and restructuring of techniques and strategies each month—often with the help of a professional. Level three: Setting a time limit (three months?) to find and accept the best job available. Two other factors are involved. First, the individual is sufficiently flexible to adjust goals not achieved without undue frustration. Second, when a goal is achieved, the individual gives himself or herself a suitable reward.

Based upon your past experience and intimate knowledge of yourself, please rate yourself on the degree of self-discipline you possess in reaching realistic goals. Consider the rating system below as a *determination scale.*

Low									High
1	2	3	4	5	6	7	8	9	10

CONSTRUCTING YOUR PROFILE

Please study the diagram below. Notice that each of the 12 categories are listed along the top. Also, notice the scale from 1 to 10 in the left-hand margin. Your job is to return to your first rating (attitude) and place the number circled in the first column at the appropriate point on the scale. When you have transferred all 12 scores to the correct columns, connect the dots and you have your PROFILE.

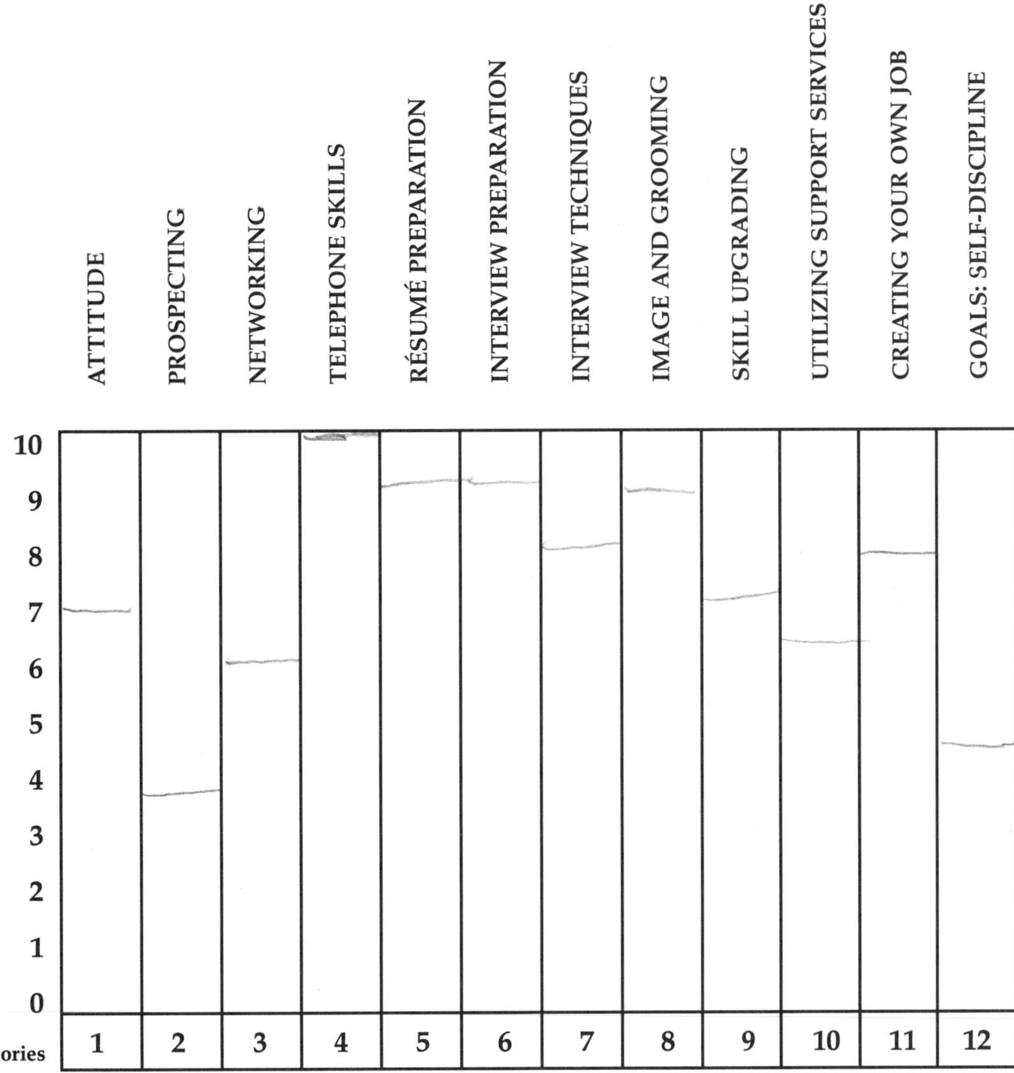

APPENDIX II

USING THE PLAN B APPROACH TO WIN THE RIGHT PART-TIME RETIREMENT JOB

A growing number of individuals over 50 have lost jobs due to the winds of change. Others are unhappy because of human conflicts and/or the downgrading of their responsibilities. Still others realize they need job involvement after retirement for either financial or psychological reasons. The result of all this is that many employees within distance of retirement need a special kind of Plan B.

> Although highly qualified in the field of printing and graphics, Lee, at 53, is finding it difficult to locate a challenging replacement. His previous position was eliminated. Result? He is developing a Plan B that will move him into retirement sooner than he and his wife had anticipated.
>
> Ruth, a widow of 60, needs to supplement her retirement income. Result? She is learning new skills and upgrading old ones to find a part-time job that will take her to 65 and Medicare coverage.
>
> Ken is 55 and under great pressure from a superior who would like nothing better than to see him retire. Result? Tired of waiting for a golden handshake, Ken is busy working on a Plan B that will provide additional retirement income through a part-time job.

Notice that neither Lee, Ruth, nor Ken *desire* a full-time job after retirement. All have a financial package sufficient to make-do, providing they can create a supplemental income that falls within their comfort zones. For many people, this is a most difficult challenge. They want to work, but not full time. They want a job, but one with less pressure. They want a position with some dignity and that will provide enough income or creative involvement to make it worthwhile. Research shows that many financially secure retirees still need some form of work to keep them challenged.

LAST CHANCE TO BE TRUE TO YOUR FUTURE

Retirement is the last chance an individual has to be true to his or her future. Finding the *right* part-time position is critical. In some cases this may mean doing a late-in-life career search to find a fresh, creative career. For example, many retirees go into business for themselves. Those who elect to work for others need all the job-finding skills of a recent college graduate. Perhaps more.

NOTHING MAKES MORE SENSE THAN USING THE SEVEN-STEP PLAN B PROCESS. For example, assume you would like to retire next year from your current job (Plan A) but will need a challenging part-time job (for either money or psychological reasons). If you return to page 28 and go through the seven steps a second time, you will see (with some variations) just how applicable the process can be to your special situation. To assist you in doing this, the seven steps are adjusted and augmented below. It is suggested you read each step in the body of the text first and then read the suggestions below.

STEP 1: COMMIT YOURSELF. Face it, you need as much support in preparing a retirement program as you do for a Plan B. Maybe more! Your best approach would be to sign up for a pre-retirement seminar (if your company does not offer one you might enroll in one at a local college). This could become a support group for you. Your Plan B effort would give your comprehensive retirement plan special help in an area where it is most needed. If married, it is strongly recommended that you work as a team with your spouse. Other support people may also be needed.

EACH STEP WORKS!

STEP 2: DO BETTER AT YOUR PRESENT JOB. There are two reasons why, as a possible retiree, you should consider streamlining your job. First, simplify things at work to get rid of some pressure. This is traditional and often expected by employers. Second, you need extra time (both on the job and at home) to do retirement planning. The more efficient you become at work, the more excited you will be about retirement! Go to it!

STEP 3: LEARN MORE FROM WHERE YOU ARE. Just because you are thinking about retirement is not a signal for you to stop learning. Just the opposite! Now is the time to learn skills from your present job that will help you qualify for a post-retirement job. Can you transfer present skills or do you need to learn new ones? What can you learn now that will help you later? It is natural for people about to retire to stop learning. This is never wise. Give this step some thought!

STEP 4: IMPROVE SKILLS YOU CAN USE AFTER RETIREMENT. Many people who retire are forced to take part-time jobs beneath their capabilities. This, of course, is free choice (some like getting away from the pressures). Most retirees, however, want a mental challenge and the financial rewards that go along with accomplishments. If this sounds like you, then the time to qualify for a new career or position is while you are still on a payroll. The way to do this, of course, is to find the job you really want ahead of time. Then start the qualification process. This is especially true if you intend to start your own business.

IT'S NEVER TOO LATE!

STEP 5: BACK TO SCHOOL? SELF-INSTRUCTION? BOTH?
More and more individuals approaching retirement are returning to college to learn new skills or bring old ones up-to-date. Some plan to turn hobbies into part-time endeavors. Others will learn skills so they can build boats, homes, or do repair work at their own pace. Still others will develop office skills so they can find part-time jobs near their homes. If a local university or community college does not offer what is needed, self-instruction is often the answer. Some will do limited moonlighting (like working as a small-appliance repair-person two or three nights per week).

STEP 6: CREATIVE NETWORKING: GET STARTED TODAY.
Everything in this step applies to a potential retiree! Although an employment agency might come up with the kind of part-time job you seek, it is unlikely because most agencies work primarily with those seeking full-time jobs. Thus it is more important for you to take the initative. Through networking and information interviews you need to determine the job situation you desire. This means maintaining your confidence and not selling yourself short because of age. Also, do not permit prospective employers to take advantage of you with lower wages than deserved or expectation of more work than is reasonable. Networking is the answer and the sooner you start the better!

STEP 7: HAVE PLAN—WILL TRAVEL. As a soon-to-be retiree, you may not want to travel (where you decide to retire is usually more important than any part-time job). Your Plan B will be the key. In keeping an information or employment interview, simply tell your contact what you plan to do. Ask if anything fits both your needs and theirs.

Of course, ''The Proof is in the Pudding.'' The seven steps provide a strategy, but only you can develop a written plan and implement it.

As you do this, you may wish to use the best-selling book *Comfort Zones; A Practical Guide to Retirement Planning* as a resource to your retirement planning. *Comfort Zones* is a complete guide to retirement (it covers both financial and emotional aspects) and can be ordered using the information in the back of this book.

NOTES

NOTES

NOTES

NOTES

NOTES

NOTES

CRISP WORLDWIDE DISTRIBUTION

English language books are distributed worldwide. Major international distributors include:

ASIA/PACIFIC

Australia/New Zealand: In Learning, PO Box 1051 Springwood QLD, Brisbane, Australia 4127
Telephone: 7-3841-1061, Facsimile: 7-3841-1580 ATTN: Messrs. Gordon

Singapore: Graham Brash (Pvt) Ltd. 32, Gul Drive, Singapore 2262
Telephone: 65-861-1336, Facsimile: 65-861-4815 ATTN: Mr. Campbell

CANADA

Reid Publishing, Ltd., Box 69559-109 Thomas Street, Oakville, Ontario Canada L6J 7R4.
Telephone: (905) 842-4428, Facsimile: (905) 842-9327 ATTN: Mr. Reid

Trade Book Stores: Raincoast Books, 8680 Cambie Street, Vancouver, British Columbia, Canada V6P 6M9.
Telephone: (604) 323–7100, Facsimile: 604-323-2600 ATTN: Ms. Laidley

EUROPEAN UNION

England: Flex Training, Ltd. 9-15 Hitchin Street, Baldock, Hertfordshire, SG7 6A, England
Telephone: 1-462-896000, Facsimile: 1-462-892417 ATTN: Mr. Willetts

INDIA

Multi-Media HRD, Pvt., Ltd., National House, Tulloch Road, Appolo Bunder, Bombay, India 400-039
Telephone: 91-22-204-2281, Facsimile: 91-22-283-6478 ATTN: Messrs. Aggarwal

MIDDLE EAST

United Arab Emirates: Al-Mutanabbi Bookshop, PO Box 71946, Abu Dhabi
Telephone: 971-2-321-519, Facsimile: 971-2-317-706 ATTN: Mr. Salabbai

SOUTH AMERICA

Mexico: Grupo Editorial Iberoamerica, Serapio Rendon #125, Col. San Rafael, 06470 Mexico, D.F.
Telephone: 525-705-0585, Facsimile: 525-535-2009 ATTN: Señor Grepe

SOUTH AFRICA

Alternative Books, Unit A3 Sanlam Micro Industrial Park, Hammer Avenue STRYDOM Park, Randburg, 2194 South Africa
Telephone: 2711 792 7730, Facsimile: 2711 792 7787 ATTN: Mr. de Haas